1- WE are free [...] in
outside of we [...]
me gui[...]

Satan - the accusor
Holy Spirit guide you
Spirit has freed me from
offending him + desire to help.
WE can do nothing

grace is what God does for
us - THE LAW is what we do for
God

died to the law die to our sin
we don't have to die to please
our own self was crucified with
him. We are Free
blood of the eternal God do for
us

Justified by faith
doing things for God. is
different than walking into
God's will
Christ is perfection of all that is
required. - He died
peach doesn't have to persist the
time - WE are free

stop trying to do it on our own

we submit to the persuasions
of God. Sin nature is dead to
us - pleasing him by doing a
thing for him - one thing Required
of us   submit to Gods persuasion
        John 6:63 Spirit gives life
    44 - no one can come til he
        is drawn to God
Making up rules   dosn't work
Submit to what he pleases
us in
when I believe in him I am
the most fruitful

Rom. 8:16
        a few words next dear father

        this day I Believe

    in you

is anything hard for the Lord

HUNGRY FOR MORE

Feasting through the Word

go Lord with you

Mark 11:22 Have faith in God

Feb. 11 - 26

Like your faith you go in peace be saved

Romans - 4 - 5
1 - 11

Kandy Persall

James 2:17 faith out with work is dead

WestBow
PRESS
A DIVISION OF THOMAS NELSON

WestBow Press books may be ordered through booksellers or by contacting:

WestBow Press
A Division of Thomas Nelson
1663 Liberty Drive
Bloomington, IN 47403
www.westbowpress.com
1-(866) 928-1240

ISBN: 978-1-4497-4263-8 (sc)
ISBN: 978-1-4497-4262-1 (hc)
ISBN: 978-1-4497-4264-5 (e)
Library of Congress Control Number: 2012905536

Printed in the United States of America
WestBow Press rev. date: 04/04/2012

For Mark

Your hunger for the Word inspires me.

CONTENTS

INTRODUCTION

So you're hungry, huh? Well, this is a great meal plan because it's one of the few on the planet that actually encourages you to eat more rather than less. How's that for the perfect diet?

Although the lessons on these pages are a culmination of my experiences spent living overseas for over twenty years, my written words aren't the most valuable part of this book. In fact, reading just my words will be somewhat like eating a meal at your favorite Chinese restaurant. You'll be hungry again in a couple of hours.

If you are honestly hungry for more, you will dig into the daily Gospel Readings before moving on to the following chapter. If you genuinely have "growl tummy," you'll stop and look up the Scripture references scattered within every lesson. And if you are really ravished, you'll direct each prayer to the Lord rather than just reading it with your eyes. Only by partaking of the Word of Life will you find the joy and delight your soul is truly hungry for (Jer. 15:16).

So tell me: did you just turn to Jeremiah 15:16? Great! Then get your chopsticks ready for quite a meal.

Jer 15:16 your words were found, + I ate them, + they became a joy and a delight to me of my heart

words

CHAPTER 1

THE REALITY OF THE WORD

Bible Reading: John 1–3

> "In the beginning was the Word, and the Word was
> with God, and the Word was God. And the Word
> became flesh, and dwelt among us" (John 1:1, 14).

Have you ever tried stuffing everything you own into a few suitcases?

Before I could move overseas, I had to do just that: cram two closets into thirteen pieces of luggage. Married seven years, Mark and I had quite the accumulation of stuff. From baby paraphernalia to wedding crystal, it seemed we had it all. For months, we packed and repacked, trying to decide how to make it all fit.

Then we discovered an answer: space-saver bags. With the body of a Ziploc and the mouth of a suction fish, these little guys allowed us to vacuum-pack a room full of stuff into one seventy-pound cinder block. Once our belongings were vacuum-sealed, I considered attaching a neon "do not disturb" sign to the latch. We'd crammed it in there. I knew what would happen if air hit the contents.

Rewind two thousand years and imagine the Father's Parcel. That was a true feat of compression. As if packing for a cosmic trip,

God compacted the Truth of the heavenlies into a microscopic spiritual seed. He folded every facet of love and every glimmer of hope into a single space-saving cell.

The omnipotent Creator of the galaxies fused with woman to become the only spiritual zygote. God came to earth in the form of a sperm. (And we worry about faith no bigger than a seed!)

Talk about a cramped overseas flight! God's Son journeyed through Mary's womb. We call Him Jesus. Heaven calls Him "the Word" (Rev. 19:13).

The word *Logos* isn't just Greek for something said, but is the Living Voice who literally spoke all of creation into existence (John 1:3). He *is* life. Stop for a moment and think about the largest mountain that you have ever seen suddenly becoming so condensed that it could fit into your wallet. This is only the beginning of what the Father's compression was like. The Maker of heaven and earth fit His every thought into newborn size.

Jesus, who created all things and was before all things, came to us in the form of a tiny bundle. Although unconstrained by time, God "shrink-wrapped" Life and placed Him in a woman's womb, where He slowly began expanding. At His birth, the Father unfolded Light and Life to us. His physical growth was nothing like the expansion of Life living out among us (John 1:4, 14). You see, God is all about Life (John 6:48).

Previously, all of God's communication had been via "letter," handwritten on stone tablets and given to Moses. Although handwritten by God, that engraving was heavy to carry and even heavier to obey. The Father knew we couldn't live by the written law. After all, we easily forget what we read. So He relocated His Son to live perfection inside us.

With the same creative energy God had used to create the heavens and earth, the Father caused Grace and Truth to assume a visual image. Through Jesus, God's Life was now generated into that which we could see, hear, and touch (1 John 1:1). The actuality of the heavenlies now had hair, teeth, and skin. With Christ, God's Word given to Moses came off the "page" and revealed the reality of God. Truth took the form of man, so that we could see what the Word looks like.

When Jesus says that He is truth, He doesn't merely mean that He is genuine or real (John 14:6). Instead, the meaning is much deeper and divine. He *is* truth—the substance and essence of God Himself.

With the push for 3-D media, television manufacturers want us to imagine ourselves within the display. They advertise images so realistic that we want to step in to interact with the actors. But envision a dimension in which characters would walk off the flat screen and into our lives. Forsaking a written script, they would relate to us personally, sharing our life as we shared theirs. We would have to set an extra plate for dinner. We'd have to have room for them in the car. Wouldn't that be amazing?

This is exactly what God did by sending Jesus Christ to earth in the form of a man. Although Jesus existed in the form of God (Phil. 2:6), He took on our image. The Word became 3-D. He stepped out of our flat-panel understanding of Him and into our living rooms.

As long as our perception of Christ revolves around rules, we limit our interaction with Him because we keep Him in the flat screen. Carefully abiding by our own self-selected commandments gives us no more freedom than the Pharisees had with their Law; "For if any kind of rule-keeping had power to create life in us, we would certainly have gotten it by this time" (Gal. 3:21, MSG).

No matter what tactic we try, "no one is justified by the Law" (Gal. 3:11). Rule-keeping never makes anyone perfect (Heb. 10:1). Yes, it sure lets you know how to recognize sin, but self-regulation has no power to overcome it (Rom. 3:20).

no human is justified by works of the law, since thru law comes knowledge of sin

That's the great thing about our 3-D Lord. When Jesus came, His personality explained exactly what truth meant. The Word sprang into Life and actually became a breathing individual: human, yet divine. Although the Word was from the beginning of time, He was one of us. God assumed a dimension that we could see and understand.

The Word became flesh for the first time within Christ. Now He desires to do so again and again, daily, within you and me. Our "religion" is not to be lived in adherence to invariable restrictions. Instead, the Life walks out of heaven and into our hearts. Our every breath should remind us of His breath of Life within. He truly is Spirit and Life (John 6:63).

Our life is to be a continuation of His every Word unfolded within each of us. Take a moment now to thank Him for His life within you and to ask Him to live out that life day by day within you. As you pray the prayer below, personalize it so that He hears your heart, not just the words.

Holy Father,

Thank You for sending Your Son, Jesus, so that we could experience You. You came in a form that we could actually see and touch (1 John 1:2). It's really too much to comprehend.

I ask that the eyes of my heart would be enlightened, so that I will recognize You daily. You've given me the same hope that You gave the early disciples. Turn my head to see the riches of glory that You mention, as well as the faith to know Your power in all Your greatness (Eph. 1:18–19).

You've never been a fan of having us very far away, huh, Lord? (Eph. 2:13). Not only have you made provision that Your family gets to live next to You in the heavenlies one day, but You also settle down within us to let us know what heaven will be like. I want to cling closely to my kingdom passport. Help me understand how best to live as a foreigner here on earth (Hebrews 11:13–16).

Allow me to unwrap a little more of Your grace and truth today (John 1:17). There is always more to Your gift than I have discovered. Thank You for being Spirit and Life within me (John 6:63). In Jesus' name, amen.

) 1:17 law thru moses, grace + truth thru Christ over lord

) 6:63 spirit gives life, flesh of no avail - the words 2 have spoken to you R spirit + life

I want to cling closely to my passport — I may need a few Visa's Lord —

Recognize God daily — shut out the accuser.

foreigner on earth

Reality of the Word

CHAPTER 2

THE SPIRIT OF THE WORD

Bible Reading: John 4–5

"God is spirit" (John 4:24).

Living in one culture and hailing from another can cause a lot of trouble. I should know; I managed to mangle every Chinese tradition in my twenty years overseas. Initially, every time that I opened my mouth to speak, I found that middle school Spanish kept creeping into my vocabulary. Because I couldn't read Chinese, I spent countless hours searching the market for the perfect potato in a sea of rice. From the words I spoke to the way I conducted myself, I didn't act very Chinese.

We find ourselves in much the same predicament when we become kingdom citizens, don't we? Our new passports show that we are children of the King, but our habits look pretty foreign. In order for the Life of Christ to be lived out within us, we must realize that we are born of the Spirit, not of the flesh.

Picture a voltage adaptor, which keeps a high-wattage outlet from frying your 110-voltage device. Multi-pronged, it will work anywhere from England, with its flat tri-pronged plug, to Kenya, with its rounded, dual one. A voltage adaptor allows us to tap into energy wherever we are.

We, as people, were also created with dual voltage. Born in the flesh, our only option is to pull our strength from the ability of our minds or passion of our emotions. We create regulations about how we will live and try to model ourselves around the lives of others. It's really quite exhausting!

Before Christ, this is the best we can do. Indeed, drawing power from the flesh is like plugging into a mechanical generator. It makes a lot of noise but produces a limited amount of energy.

Although you still have the option of fleshly generator living, you also don't have to live that way. The Presence of the Holy Spirit means that you no longer are relegated to just try harder. His overflow of Power pulsates a new ability to surge with divine nature (2 Pet. 1:3–4).

When Christ enters our spirits by faith, a whole new Power source becomes available to us. Our faith connection opens the door of the Word, which reveals an entire power grid in our inner man. Jesus, our adaptor, reconnects us to our high-voltage God.

Okay, so how do we live that out?

The goal is not to get closer to God. We are not climbing some spiritual ladder in which we take two steps up and fall three rungs down. We've tried this approach and it leaves us exhausted and disappointed.

This very minute is what is important. Are you plugged into Him now? Have you faithed Him for the moment? "Faithe" is a verb of action, not of option. Let's use this archaic spelling throughout our study to remind us of this very fact. The decision to abide right now is the absolute most that you can do. It's not about how you will live tomorrow, but where you set your purpose just now.

Plugged into Christ this very moment, energizes you with the power source you were created for. As you turn to faithe Him, He receives you instantly. And in the blink of an eye, you are walking in the Spirit. The flow of the Father is immediate, not something you work into (Rom. 9:16). *depends on Gods mercy not the will of man* When we flip the light switch on in our living room, our concern (if any) is about whether or not the light illuminates. We rarely even think about whether or not it will come on tomorrow. Our concern is the flow of current at that moment.

Our connection with Christ should be the same way. He connects our spirit to a constant flow of energy—His Spirit to our spirit, moment by moment. In fact, as we listen in spirit, we will find that His Spirit is actually testifying with our spirit that we are His children (Rom. 8:16). When the Spirit of God lives in us, we don't have to live by the dictation of the physical realm (Rom. 8:9).

Today, in John 4:24, you read, "God is spirit." Since He *is* Spirit, He connects to you in that way. Relax. Believe Him. The Energy of His Kingdom can live in you from the inside out.

Listen how Hannah Whitall Smith describes this change: "I have noticed that wherever someone has been truly faithful following the Lord, several things have inevitably followed sooner or later. Meekness and quietness of spirit in time become the characteristics of the daily life. A submissive acceptance of the will of God is shown as it comes in the hourly events of each day. There is a willingness in the believer whose life is in the hands of God to suffer all the good pleasure of His will. There is a sweetness when provoked [sic]. There is a calmness in the midst of turmoil. There is a yielding to the wishes of others, and an insensibility to slights and affronts. There is an absence of worry or anxiety. There is a deliverance from care and fear. All these, and many other similar graces, are invariably found to be the natural outward development of that inward life which is hid with Christ in God."[1]

---

1   Hannah Whitall Smith, *The Christian's Secret to a Happy Life* (New Kensington, PA: Whitaker House, 1983), 189–190.

R. Spirit of the word

As you regularly "faithe" the flow, you will find that His Word inside you becomes as fluent as your mother tongue. You may want to leave yourself spiritual flashcards so you can saturate yourself in His language. Hannah, my daughter, has scripture cards taped in prominent places around her home. My friend Carrie writes a new verse every week on her kitchen whiteboard and finds ways to discuss it with her children as they eat and play. It's not the method that's important; it's your focus.

You are an individual whose passport is now issued by God's Kingdom of redeemed saints from all over the world. Your entry visa is stamped by the original Minister of the Interior. It bears unlimited, irrevocable entry as you live in Him and He lives in you. Ask Him to plug you into that truth throughout your day.

Holy Father,

All that You have done for me amazes me. You exchanged my life—both past and present—for the life of Christ, Your Son (2 Cor. 5:21). I'm not only a passport holder of a new Kingdom but I am also recognized in the heavenlies as bearing royal blood (John 1:12).

I have to admit to You that I spend entirely too much time living off the battery power of the flesh. Because I have allowed myself to be so turned onto this earthly culture, I allow the temptations of my flesh, my eyes, and my ego to make my daily decisions (1 John 2:16). You've caught me with a new pack of AAAs in hand. Forgive me.

Since You have already provided me with a new identity, I want to act accordingly (2 Cor. 5:17). Allow me to fix my eyes upon Your Son, who has already modeled just what it looks like to be a Kingdom walker on a worldly terrain (Eph. 2:10). I choose today to be plugged into Christ as my energy source. Accomplish whatever that means as I wait on You (Ps. 138:8). In Jesus' name, Amen.

I chose this day to be willing to be willing

CHAPTER 3

THE LIFE IN THE WORD

Bible Reading: John 6–7

> "This is the work of God, that you believe in Him whom He has sent" (John 6:29).

Even before arriving in Taiwan, Mark and I decided that learning Chinese was essential. If we were going to communicate with anybody, then we needed to set our hearts on learning Mandarin. So, while still in jet lag, we enrolled in a language school and began study. We even hired an "amah" to watch our preschool girls, so that I could attend class full-time to learn the proper tones of our new language.

After class, I would sit in the floor with the girls and my flashcards, trying to play "baby dolls" one moment and memorize tones the next. Four-year-old Hannah would often put her little hand over my mouth, begging me to stop the torture. "Just speak English, Mommy," she would plead. I can only imagine what my teacher thought as I distorted Mandarin with my Texas accent. Nevertheless, for the next two years, I juggled the tasks of language school, family life, and cultural adaptation. It was quite the balancing act.

In our Christian life, we often wonder what our full-time job is to be. Shall I focus on evangelism, prayer, or Bible study? Shall I facilitate a video series or volunteer at the local food bank? Just what is God's will for my life?

Here in John 6:29, we find the secret of laboring for God. Read it again with me: "This is the work of God, that you believe ..." Faith is the only real spiritual work that we can do for God. In fact, He values faith so highly, that when He inventories our faith, He equates it to righteousness (Rom. 4:3). We are justified by faith not by works (Gal. 2:16).

Doubting this truth is like unplugging from the source of our power. The Power Grid is still within us, but we choose not to receive the flow. The choice is ours. We may connect with His life through faith or allow doubt to leave us hanging (Matt. 9:29). It's up to us. Believing should be our daily occupation.

Let's walk through one day with faith as your chief objective. As you rise from your bed, while still groggy from sleep, you speak first to Him. Give Him the plans of your day, as well as your emotions, thoughts, and reactions. Before the day has progressed too far, open His Word to see what He will say to you. You may have to get up a little earlier before heading to work or have audio scriptures available on your iPod if you're running late. If you are at home, it's okay to allow your baby to wait in the crib a few more minutes or continue your quiet time in front of your children as they eat their breakfast. Regardless of your situation, you can communicate with the Father in the midst of others. Jesus did (Luke 9:18).

Realize that any verse that seems to stand out is His voice calling to you. As the Holy Spirit prompts, stop reading and ask the Lord to show you how to fulfill what He has said actively. Jot down notes to refer to later.

Let's say your passage includes Philippians 4:6. Maybe the Holy Spirit impresses you to "be anxious for nothing." You realize that you are often anxious about your life and worry about many things. You see a cross-reference in your Bible and read Psalm 37:8, "Do not fret; it leads only to evildoing." Wow! You are silenced, thinking about the significance of these two verses upon your life.

Next, a verse fragment pops into your mind: "Do not be worried about your life." If you are like me, you will immediately begin to worry that you can't remember where that verse is found and wonder what the rest of it says. Scribble down a note to yourself to find that reference later.

For now, the work is to believe that the Lord is speaking to you. He is speaking! Rest in the fact; He has fulfilled all requirements on your life (Eph. 2:14; Rom. 8:4).

During the day, several things will probably happen to cause you to have uneasy feelings. But, each time you begin to feel anxious, say a quiet, short prayer. Ask God to keep reminding you of His peace rather than the anxiety of the moment.

As you continue through the day, use Philippians 4:6 as your "faithing" verse for the day. Say it aloud as you can. Let your mind wash with this truth, allowing Him to add verses or songs into your thoughts. Never take for granted random praise songs or snatches of verses. Sometimes, I even ask Him what song is currently on His "playlist" and ask that He download it into my spirit. Allow Him to be your Holy "Rememberer" (John 14:26).

Jesus promises, "It shall be done to you according to your faith" (Matt. 9:29). Our response should be, "May it be done to me according to your word" (Luke 1:38). People who believe are just filled with blessings (Luke 1:45).

On one particular trip back to the United States, I was inundated with all of the adorable decor items in every store. Knowing I had only a few weeks to shop, I found myself wanting a little of everything that I saw. Realistically, neither my budget nor my luggage could accommodate such a desire.

As I prayed about this one morning, the Lord impressed me with a verse fragment from childhood: "The LORD is my shepherd, I shall not want" (Ps. 23:1). I knew this to be Him speaking directly to me. From that point on, I found many instances to talk with Him about that verse.

My remaining shopping trips went something like this: "I sure do want that, Lord. Show me how having a shepherd is better than having it. My 'want-er' is working overtime just now, Father. Could You shepherd me into contentment?"

He faithfully walked with me each time I asked, and I found I went home to Taiwan more fulfilled than ever before.

Don't obsess about your failures. These will happen, because stumbling is a given (James 3:2). God, who placed you into an evil world, also has a plan as to how you can overcome evil with good. Praise Him, for when you are weak, He is strong (2 Cor. 13:9).

Remember, He is your 3-D God; He came "off the screen" and into your life. As you focus on Him, He will begin to pour out thoughts of Himself and increase your faith. He is pleased by faith, not random activity (Heb. 11:6).

Unlike all other lovers, our God uses spiritual methods to reach us. When we believe that the Scriptures, songs, and Spirit promptings in our heart are Jesus' advances toward us, our spirits are strengthened to more easily recognize Him the next time. Let's make believing in Him our chief goal today. _Him who died 4 me_

Holy Father,

Thank You for allotting a measure of faith to me (Rom. 12:3). Without it, there would be no way that I could ever begin to believe in what I cannot see. Yet, I know that the same faith

life 13 _of the word_

that You gave me initially is meant to grow daily as I look for You (Eph. 2:8; Rom. 4:20).

The problem is that all too often I get involved in what I can see around me without considering the magnitude of what I have in the heavenlies. My desire is to faithe You, so I ask that You increase my ability to believe (Luke 17:5). Not only do I want to please You, but I also want to watch life daily unfold according to Your Word, not according to my own doubt (Luke 1:38; Matt. 9:29). Obviously, I need You to spill out of me. Go for it. Okay? In Jesus' name, Amen.

CHAPTER 4

THE REVELATION OF THE WORD

Bible Reading: John 8–9

> "He who is of God hears the words of God"
> (John 8:47).

My great appreciation for the emperor penguin came on one of those long overseas flights. While others watched *King Kong,* I sat spellbound as *March of the Penguins* unfolded in French with English subtitles. When our plane landed some ten hours later, I had a new understanding of our Creator.

Here is what I learned:

The adult male penguin assumes care of a newly-laid egg so that his mate can begin her fifty-mile trek to feed in open water. During her absence, prospective fathers huddle together against the Antarctic winter. With winds and temperature well below freezing, they endure the sixty-five-day fast with a single egg balanced atop their feet. Should the egg roll onto the frozen ground, it freezes and dies within seconds.

Days after the chicks hatch, the females return in droves to undertake responsibility for the newborn. Yet, even before reaching the site where father and chick await, the mother begins to call out to her own little family; soon, the decibel level of the peaceful snowcap increases to rock-concert intensity. Amazingly, despite the screeching din, each family reunites as they recognize one another's cry.

If a penguin can find her chick, why do we think our God would do less? He too, speaks specifically to His own offspring. When He gave you the right to be called His, He also gave you the right to hear from Him (John 8:47). This is part of His adoption plan. As His child, we recognize His voice because He opens our ears (John 10:3, 27). The psalmist child even asked the Father to "dig" out his ears in order that he hear clearly (Ps. 40:6); not a bad prayer for us as well.

It is God's desire that we hear Him. So much so, that He even promises to tell us what's to come next (John 16:13). Although His thoughts are higher than ours are, we should expect to hear from Him on a regular, daily basis. *GREATER love has no*

man than He lay down His life 4

We become bogged down when we listen for His voice with our *HIS* minds or emotions. Because He is Spirit, interaction with Him *FRIENDS* must be spiritual as well (John 4:24). His voice will always speak to us Spirit to spirit: His Spirit to ours (Rom. 8:16). He reveals His Word to our spirit, and then, in time, our thoughts and emotions will know His message as well (Matt.16:17).

Because spiritual communication is a foreign concept to us, the Father sent His Holy Spirit to live within us as our personal translator. The Word sets up residence within our spirit. He breathes the *pneuma* of His Spirit, or the holy "breath," into us so that we may recognize Him through spiritual disclosure (Eph. 1:17). *THE GOD Has given me the spirit of revelation + knowledge of Christ*

Each day, as we read His Word, we approach His Presence *HIS SON* somewhat as the priests of old entered into the temple. There, in our own "holy of holies," we present the written word to the Word of Life Himself. No longer do we read the Bible seeking to "get something" out of it. Instead, we bring the Living Word to the feet of the Life-Giver. Fused together, the Word is no longer something that we just read, but is He who lives within us. As we daily practice this spiritual reading, our eyes will be opened to recognize Him (Luke 24:31). His wisdom to understand the Scripture will spill from our spirit into our minds and emotions (Luke 24:45).

Word is HE who lives with in us

As you believe in Jesus, use your voice to agree with all that He has said. Even the Hebrew word for *meditate* includes a connotation of speaking out one's thoughts. But make that announcement more than just words. Make Him your purpose for life. As you speak out His Word, those words take action in power. Speak out your confidence in Jesus and then go on to allow His truths to change your life: "Therefore as you have received Christ Jesus the Lord, so walk in Him" (Col. 2:6).

Read the following statements of faith aloud to Him, pausing in-between sentences so that He can respond if He chooses:

- Christ, I believe that You desire to speak to me.
- I believe that You have given me the capacity to hear the spiritual Word.
- I believe that I can come to recognize Your Voice.
- I believe that Your Word has power, not just syllables.
- I believe that You are transforming my life.

Today, before you open the Word, ask Him to enlighten your spiritual eyes to see the life of the Word. Pray that He removes the veil of human interpretation and energizes you to live the Word, rather than just know *about* the words. Give Him authority to live out His Word within you. He knows how.

LIVE THE WORD

Holy Father,

Thank You for giving me the ears to hear Your Word and for speaking to me, Spirit to spirit (John 8:47; Rom. 8:16). You have warned me that I should be careful what I listen to (Mark 4:24), but I confess that often, I am too busy listening to the clamor of

Jn 8:47 He who is of God Hears the word of God

Rom 8:16 it is the spirit of God bearing witness with our spirit — We R spirit children of GOD

MARK 4:24 & take Heed what u Hear. The measure u give will Be u The measure

17

the world rather than to Your still small voice (1 Kings 19:12–13). Please forgive me. *God in the still small voice, what r U doing here?*

For so long, I've read Your Word depending on my emotions to speak more than You. I felt if my heart trembled, I had done something right. But if I didn't feel a special tug, I figured I had done something wrong. Forgive me for thinking that my connection with You depends on how I feel. *NOT ABOUT ME*

As I place my hand on a copy of Your written Word, I recognize that this print version gives voice to You, who are the living version. With You in my spirit and the printed Word in my lap, You desire to fill every space in-between. As I read the written Word, I am giving You permission to speak.

I desire to tune into You, so that despite what goes on around me, I can always know Your promised peace (John 16:33). Give me the patience to wait on You, so that the song within me will spring forth (Ps. 40:1–3). Praise You for all that You have already done for me. No one compares to You (2 Sam. 7:22). In Jesus' name, Amen. *NO ONE LIKE U*

it isn't about me

Be still

CHAPTER 5

LISTENING TO THE WORD

Bible Reading: John 10–12

"And the sheep hear His voice" (John 10:3).

Despite the darkness of our seventh-floor apartment, Mark and I were determined to find our daughters. The floor beneath us continued to jump and jolt as we blindly felt our way down the familiar hallway. Although we had experienced several tremors in our previous nine years, we knew this one was a full-blown earthquake.

Mark took the longer path to find Hannah while I searched for Hilary's door. As I gripped the handle, I realized that something had fallen against her door from the other side. With superhuman strength I had only read about, I forced aside the debris wedged between my daughter and me. In the dripping darkness, I called to Hilary, hoping intently to hear her voice.

With the childlike faith of her eleven years, Hilary responded from her top bunk, "I'm fine, Mom. I'm just hanging on and praising Jesus."

Although I couldn't see Hilary, I knew she was okay by the sound of her voice. From her tone, I could tell that she was frightened, but unharmed. As I stumbled toward her, she climbed down and together we went to find Mark and Hannah.

When we cannot see clearly, our sense of hearing is heightened. Being in darkness increases our dependence upon sound. I can hear, even when I cannot see.

Christ likened His disciples to sheep in John 10, emphasizing the audible rather than the visual. He said that His sheep would hear His voice because He knew that sometimes seeing the Shepherd would be far too difficult. If we are diligent to beat a path to Him frequently while there is light, we will still be able to hear our way to Him in the dark.

Why would Christ bother to say that He wanted to speak to us if He didn't believe that we would have the capacity to hear Him? We can know His voice because He has promised that we will hear His Word (John 8:47). The reason that we so often read the Word without really hearing Him is that we don't really want to obey what He says. When we make a deliberate decision to follow what He says, we can't help but hear the Spirit's voice.

Reading the Word should never be an information-gathering exercise. In fact, we are told specifically not to lean on our own understanding (Prov. 3:5). We must hear His voice not only with spiritual ears but also by allowing the Spirit inside of us to do the interpretation. *Trust in the Lord not on your own knowledge*

The reason our quiet times "don't last" is because this intentional time with the Lord is just a portion of the time we need with Him each day. He doesn't give us everything in a few minutes, just as you don't eat enough breakfast to last all day. Like a spiritual IV, the Word is to drip into your mind and heart moment by moment. This doesn't mean you *do* something different. It means you *believe* Someone—the Lord—is different. He is about relationship, not rules.

In almost every flight we take, we notice someone sporting a pair of Bose headphones. Billed as the desire of every traveler, their noise-canceling technology was created to block all external noise, while allowing the listener to hear delicate nuances of their preferred sound. Living in the Spirit is like wearing flesh-canceling headphones.

Wearing His headphones cannot be achieved by a method or a program. It only comes from having a daily connection with Him. You can expect silence between spiritual tracks. Silence creates anticipation toward the next portion of life. Yet it's not the silence that you anxiously await, but the voice of the Spirit.

This is a whole new way to live. No longer trying and striving in darkness, but moment by moment hearing from Jesus and obeying what He says. God has set us free to live a life of fullness for Him.

His voice magnetically draws us toward Him. He has freed us to walk in innocence rather than living in guilt (Rom. 8:1–2). "If you are being led by the Spirit, you are not under the Law" (Gal. 5:18).

In this walk of freedom, He speaks to us moment by moment—Spirit to spirit. As we learn to hear Him, He literally changes our desires to match His. Although we can't see Him, let's move toward His voice and trust Him to do what He says (Ps. 37:4–5).

Holy Father,
    Praise You as the God of all light and antithesis of all darkness (1 John 1:5). Amazingly enough, just being Light isn't enough for You. You actively take light to the dark places, calling to us, so that we too can live in light (1 Pet. 2:9). The flame of Your life kindles the wicks of our hearts.
    As we each shakily carry our own candle, we soon find that it is only by following You that it stays lit. Turning to follow You

is the only way to keep in the light (Ps. 36:9). May the fragrance of my candle emit a pleasing aroma to You.

As You know, there are still times that I don't see Light. In fact, sometimes You seem to be a God who actually tries to hide Himself from my sight (Isa. 45:15). These ways of Yours are far out of the realm of my understanding (Isa. 55:9). So, what can I do but continue to feel my way through the darkness to that place where I last saw You? As I do this, don't forget that You have promised that nothing is hidden that won't be revealed (Mark 4:22). I really need You to show up.

Change my desires into those You have for me. I want to delight in You and find my heart desire equal to Yours (Ps. 37:4). So, today, whether I find myself seeing clearly or not, I choose to trust You. Reveal Yourself to me, moment by moment, so that I may follow in freedom. In Jesus' name, Amen.

Holy spirit

I am Vine you
are branches
branches bear
fruit

CHAPTER 6

FOLLOWING THE WORD

Bible Reading: John 13–16

> "Lord, we do not know where You are going,
> how do we know the way?" (John 14:5).

After a few years of Chinese study, my Canadian friend and I decided we needed a break. A local expat group was hosting a women's retreat and we made plans to attend. "We can take our car," I announced bravely. "I'll drive, and you read the map."

Now the map was in Mandarin, but as Julia and I pored over it, we realized that we recognized the characters on most of the city streets. We each owned a Taiwan driver's license and were experienced at nosing our way into the most congested traffic. This would be a piece of mooncake.

As we left the city limits, truth dawned that the map was not to scale and we fast became lost. After far too many turns, we began to disagree on the best way to our destination. Confused and shaken, we pulled into a small Taiwanese shop. I opened the door and in muddled Mandarin I announced, "I. Am. Late!"

Having no idea what I'd just said, two amused men looked up from their tea. Their wide grin exposed reddened teeth, stained from Taiwan's chewing tobacco substitute, betel nut. Not only

23

was there that, but their response to me came in an altogether different Chinese dialect as well. I began to have an out-of-body panic. Pulling out the map, I began my signs and wonders approach.

Light dawned and one of the men began to smile and chatter pleasantly. As he saw my blank stare, he motioned me out the door and into my car, where Julia had been prayerfully waiting. Within moments, he was on his Vespa scooter, signaling for us to follow. For ten of the longest minutes of my life, we twisted up hairpin mountain roads, before recognizing the sign we'd been searching for. With a wave, our guide left us at the camp entrance and began his descent, smiling ear to ear.

When Thomas asked about the way in John 14:5, he was asking for a map of clear directions leading to Jesus' next destination. Thomas wanted to know the "where," so that he could decide on the "how." Instead, Jesus answered his question with a "Who."

As we journey with the Lord, our natural tendency is to ask for an atlas detailing the path, so that we may decide when to make appropriate stops and detours. We don't mind the ports of call. We would just like to plan the sailing route.

"Where are we going?" we ask.

"That would be toward Me," He replies. "Come on!"

Following after Him, we find that He is not only the actual channel by which we find our destination; He *is* the destination. In Him, we not only find out how to know God; we also find God Himself. He is both the Way *and* the Truth (John 14:6).

This Truth is not just factual and right, although this is a part of Jesus being truth. He is both the reality and actuality of God. The writer of Hebrews described Christ as the "exact representation of (God's) nature" (Hebrews 1:3). As we follow Him, we see God. Although we wait for Him along the journey, we don't have to wait until heaven to see Him. He gives us glimpses all along the way.

To top it off, Jesus proclaims that He is also the Life. In Greek, it is as if He is saying, "I am not only the accessibility to and reality of God; I am your vitality in God." Jesus emphasizes these three characteristics as connected one to the other. In finding one, you are on your way to discovering another.

Practically, it's much easier to follow a guy on a scooter than it is to follow the one who is Spirit. "How can we know the way?" Herein is where the quiet time of daily silence before Him comes in. We know that he who is of God hears Him (John 8:47). We can also be assured that if the Spirit of God is within us, our spirit is alive to receive Him, see Him, and even live Him (Rom. 8:9–11). Remember, it's not about a formula conceived with the mind. It's about voluntarily moving your desires underneath His and yielding to His steps. We do it once for His sake, then over and over again for our own.

Set aside twenty minutes to spend in quiet before Him today. Begin with the prayer below, asking Him to focus your mind on Him. Then, meditate on the Lord as your way, your truth, and your life. Allow these three characteristics to rest in your spirit and soul. Wait between each characteristic for Him to speak any new revelation that He may have for you. Then, begin again. When your mind wanders (and it will), ask Him to bring you back before Him. I believe in you. He does too.

Holy Father,

I realize that I have no idea how best to allow You to be my way, truth, and life (John 14:6). I am so accustomed to following a program or procedure that I have no clue how to retrain myself to do anything differently. How can I be set free from going back to using the same formula of religion that I've failed at again and again (Rom. 7:24)?

I need You. I need You to lead me beside You in quietness and restore my very busy soul (Ps. 23:2–3). I don't even know where

I am Free — step out of the box

to begin, but believing that You are the Way, I stand before You, ready to follow.

With this very prayer, I tremble. I know myself and am afraid that I'll only stumble back into familiar paths. Strengthen my feeble knees and give me a straight path for my feet (Heb. 12:12–13). Remind me often that You are the God of peace who has equipped us to please You (Heb. 13:20–21).

I stand here before You, seeking and asking You to reveal Yourself, so that I may follow (Jer. 6:16). This journey must be a spiritual one; one that takes place by faith and not by sight (2 Cor. 5:7). Give me the faith to follow as Abraham did, following the *Who* without knowing the *where* (Heb. 11:8). Draw me along this path with Your magnetic power and whisper often in my innermost ear that I may know of Your presence (John 6:44; Isa. 30:21). Take my hand and let's get started. In Jesus' name, Amen.

CHAPTER 7

THE INFLUENCE OF THE WORD

Bible Reading: John 17–21

> "You gave [Me] authority over all flesh" (John 17:2).

The week had been incredibly long. Not only had the noise and odors of three million people crowded my space, but I had also just spent a worthless week in Chinese class studying "A Trip to the Zoo." Mark decided it was time to take me out of the city—and fast.

Preschoolers in tow, we headed to Yang Ming Mountain, a nearby green space that promised quiet. As we arrived underneath a canopy of trees, my pulse slowed and my breathing deepened. This was going to be exactly what I needed.

Only a few other families milled about, and we found a private corner in which to stake claim. I spread out our blanket and unpacked our picnic lunch. Soon we were peacefully munching away on our sandwiches and listening to the relative quiet of our location.

The solitude didn't last.

Because of the Chinese cultural view of comfort in numbers, our secluded location was soon deemed prime. At first, I ignored the comments regarding Hannah's blond ringlets and our peanut butter sandwiches. But as family after family moved their "bien dang" box lunches next to ours, I erupted in my best Chinese:

"Do we look like zoo animals to you? Stop staring at us! Do I look like a mother monkey with her babies?"

In retrospect, I'm sure that my screeching sounded just like the very scenario I'd been so vehemently denouncing. I had used my vocabulary words, but somehow I didn't feel like telling my teacher about the experience.

Although it was admittedly one of my worst outbursts, I found I continued to cycle between pious prayers in the mornings and hormonal outbursts in the afternoons. Being in a foreign environment always seemed to squeeze the very worst out of me. Where was the power of the Lord to curb such emotional tirades?

Sometimes we have to see ourselves as we really are before we can trust the Lord to be who He is. Although Jesus was given authority over all fleshliness, our church pews are filled with Christians who don't live like it (John 17:2). We hold passports to the Kingdom, but spend most of our time vacationing in the flesh.

As long as we continue holding the right to our own lives, we will continue to fail in all areas of our personality, including our emotions. Indeed our spirits are willing, but our flesh remains weak (Matt. 26:41). Our desires must be returned to their Creator: the only One who can truly control them.

As a woman, I continue to deal with far too many emotions. I had the list memorized from Titus 2:5, but the sensible and pure stuff seemed to fit a stodgy disposition rather than someone who likes to laugh as much as I do. Yet, the Lord revealed that this

Titus 2:5 BE sensible chaste domestic, kind + submissive to Husband admonition to "be sensible" had nothing to do with reading glasses and frowns, but everything to do with giving Him control. The English word translated as "sober" is actually derived from a blend of two Greek words meaning "to safely rein in the feelings." Then how do I safely put on the brakes when my emotions are spinning out of control?

When my emotions overwhelm, I am tempted to think, "Well, I can't help it. That's just who I am." Yet, wasn't I supposed to be this amazing victor through Christ (Rom. 8:37)? Indeed, I have great comfort in knowing that I have every right to capture emotions and bring them to His feet. I bring Him the feelings and give Him the right to control them.

Alone, I cannot adequately control my own thoughts or emotions. I may keep them in check for a time, but eventually a situation will occur that will tear down my best-laid plans for endurance. When self is in charge of the control, I don't have much self-control.

Giving Him the emotion, as well as the right to deal with it, places the full responsibility of my actions on Him. When I recognize the surge of emotions welling within me, I pray, "Lord, I feel (anger) stirring within me. I submit my feelings to You knowing that You have all authority over them. (Anger), you are now no longer given rule over my emotions. All feelings must first check in with my Lord before reaching me."

Not only does the Lord have authority over our feelings, but He is also actually greater than the sum total of every emotion every single woman can conjure up. Men, wouldn't you agree that is really ginormous? Amazing as it seems, He is "greater than our heart" (1 John 3:20).

Even if we are not radically aware of any immediate change in our emotions, He is larger than all we can think of or imagine. The God of the galaxies is definitely bigger than the changing winds of emotions. He has the dominion.

The Holy Spirit is at work in our spirits, even when our emotions do not yet feel His effect. Wisdom comes to the hidden part of the spirit before spilling out into our emotions and mind (Ps. 51:6). The One to whom we have submitted is greater than all the situations around us. As we wait upon Him, He will reveal to our thoughts and feelings just what He is already doing in our spirits (Dan. 2:22). *as we wait*

Our hearts have the tendency to condemn us. However, God is greater than those accusations, because He envisions the bigger picture. He knows that truth agrees with final reality, not with our perception of that reality. We are to look "not at the things which are seen, but at the things which are not seen" (2 Cor. 4:18). Therein lies truth (Isa. 11:3; 2 Cor. 5:7).

Curb your speech today by deleting the words "I feel" from your vocabulary. Erasing these two words off your tongue will drain their provoking power by depleting their authority. An Arabian proverb says, "When you have spoken the word, it reigns over you. When it is unspoken you reign over it." Because your feelings are not always in agreement with the truth of His Word, purge yourself from speaking from emotions rather than from final reality. Remember you are not looking for personal perfection, but for Christ's transformation.

I feel erased gone

Holy Father,

Thank You that You are the God who is not only near to us but also literally within us (Phil. 4:5; Rom. 10:8). We need to be reminded of Your Presence daily. In fact, if Your Presence doesn't go with us, then there is absolutely no reason that we move on. Lead us to know Your Presence that we may rest therein (Exod. 33:14–15).

I'm often overwhelmed with surging emotions. Sometimes, they come with the force of the tempestuous sea, crashing and flooding the bow of my vessel. Yet, I know that You calm the waves with Your Word (Mark 4:39). You commanded, "Hush

it isn't about me or how I feel

and be still" and it was done. In the same way, I ask that You mute and muzzle my emotions, Lord, for the glory of Your name.

Don't forget, Father, that You gave Your Son authority over all flesh (John 17:2). That includes the fleshliness of my emotions. So, therefore, since You are the exact representation of God's nature (Heb. 1:3), bind up my emotions just as they are already bound in heaven (Matt. 18:18). Your Word is forever settled in heaven (Ps. 119:89), so go ahead and release the reality of the heavenlies into me right now.

Give me the strength to deal with daily failures, without wavering in unbelief (Rom. 4:20). Some days, I obey both the law of the flesh and the law of the Spirit all in the same day (Rom. 7:25). Change me from dwelling on the sin into walking in the Spirit.

Thank You that even though I continue to stumble in many ways (James 3:2), You don't condemn me (Rom. 8:1). Help me to fix my eyes on Jesus, not where I am in the progress (Heb. 12:2). Make me Christ-centered, not self-centered. In Jesus' name, Amen.

JESUS A*

It is not about me

"It's about unconditional love

LOVE

if Christ not in us no need to move on

Hush + B Still

CHAPTER 8

THE LEADING OF THE WORD

Bible Reading: Matthew 1–5

"Then Jesus was led up by the Spirit" (Matt. 4:1).

Grandsons!

Noisy, yet quiet. Peanut butter sticky, yet Johnson's & Johnson clean. Bouncing and jumping, yet cuddly in my lap. They coo. We smile. They roll. We applaud. They crawl. And we get down in the floor and crawl with them.

Oh, and when they walk. Pudgy hands grasp our weathered fingers. Our backs ache at supporting them in their first steps. Yet, with joy indescribable, we lure with arms outstretched, ready to catch a fall or encourage one more step.

Just as we coax our little ones to walk, the Spirit encourages us day by day to follow His lead. A lot of bouncing, crawling, and edging around the spiritual furniture precedes true walking in the Spirit. Before God's child can stand erect in the Spirit, she must first also learn to fall into His arms.

Our rounded spiritual feet begin the process by bobbing up and down with the decision to give Christ influence over our decisions. Just as a four-month-old can lock his or her knees to give the appearance of leg strength, our initial stand may look rather impressive. Yet, the spiritual walk is never a matter of outward appearance, but always an inward sequence of pro-spirit/anti-flesh choices. The Spirit-filled life may begin either by a mighty "rushing wind" experience, or by a quiet act of complete surrender. Either way, it is continued by the same method—choice by choice follow-through.

We say that we want the Spirit to guide our path, but then again, we also want to retain the right to make our own choices. We want to practice selective obedience. Remember, "no one can serve two masters" (Matt. 6:24). A Spirit-walker cannot leave the flesh an option. Instead, with every step, we must say with Christ: not my will, but Yours be done (Matt. 26:39).

Paul gives us a practical synopsis in Galatians 5:16 when he says, "walk by the Spirit, and you will not carry out the desire of the flesh." When we think of a child's first steps, there is a lot of stumbling and falling before the actual walking. Some babies pull up on the coffee table before lunging into nearby arms and others raise themselves up into a full stand from sitting. The process of walking is different for each.

One of the greatest distractions between crawling and walking is what the child can put in his mouth in the meantime. Just like our grandsons, the further off the ground you are, the less likely you will eat dirt. When you are busy walking in the Spirit, you don't have time to accomplish fleshly desires.

The success or failure of walking in the Spirit doesn't depend on a straight A report card, because walking in the Spirit doesn't mean keeping the Law. Unfortunately, we have believed the devil's lie that says if we are truly Spirit-filled, then we have no more struggle against sin. We somehow believe that the more mature we are in our belief, the less we will grapple with temptation.

If this is the case, then why did Jesus agonize so in the garden of Gethsemane (Luke 22:44)? Why did His prayers and supplications include loud crying and tears (Heb. 5:7)? And, after several amazing missionary journeys, why did the apostle Paul speak of not yet having obtained perfection (Phil. 3:12)? Success depends not upon a record of perfection but instead upon a willingness to both follow and repent.

Our victory is not that we never sin again. Until we see Him in eternity, the fleshly tares of our life will continue to live side by side with our spiritual man. The triumph is not how we are doing, but what He has already done! He doesn't condemn us for our weakness (Rom. 7:25–8:2). We will stumble in many ways, but as we rely on Him, we can walk as if we had never tripped (James 3:2; Romans 5:1).

We've learned with Paul that Christ's "power is perfected in weakness" (2 Cor. 12:9). What better way to keep us weak than by allowing continued temptation? We will hear His voice enough to increase our faith and stumble enough to keep us humble.

Busy yourself looking at Jesus, not your own feet. Just as a toddler is bound to fall if he begins to stare at his own Velcro-strapped shoes, you will stumble if you always focus on your own progress. Why do we spend so much time reflecting about our own actions and so little reflecting on Christ?

Jesus was led by the Spirit because He paid attention to where the Spirit was going. Did you recognize the leading of the Spirit yesterday? Today, look for evidences of His movement and find someone to talk about it with. He's always at work, you know, and that includes within you (John 5:17).

Holy Father,

What an amazing parent You are! When my spiritual feet are rounded and unstable, You get on the floor and coax me Your way. When I'm afraid to take the stairs to the heavenlies, You grasp my hand (Isa. 41:10). When I'm too tired to make another move, You pick me up and carry me awhile (Isa. 40:11). Thank You for leading me by Your Spirit (Gal. 5:18).

As my day unfolds, I pray that I would set my mind on You and thus know life and peace (Rom. 8:6). I know that those who are according to the Spirit are those who set their minds on the things of the Spirit (Rom. 8:5). Make this my determined purpose (1 Cor. 2:2). Thank You that life doesn't depend upon works, but upon You, the One who calls (Rom. 9:11).

Thank You for giving me the mind of Christ (1 Cor. 2:16). Reveal to me all that You have freely given me (1 Cor. 2:12). Grant me diligence to daily fix my eyes upon You, in order that, from this position of rest, You may lead me forward (Heb. 12:2; Heb. 4:10; Rom. 8:14). In Jesus' name, Amen.

eyes upon Christ
not upon me — if
I see Christ + can
follow HIM.

not what we are doing but what he
has already done —

CHAPTER 9

THE AUTHORITY OF THE WORD

Bible Reading: Matthew 6–9

> "'Everyone who hears these words of Mine and acts on them, may be compared to a wise man.' … When Jesus had finished these words, the crowds were amazed at His teaching; for He was teaching them as one having authority, and not as their scribes" (Matt. 7:24, 28–29).

My eyes adjusted slowly to the darkness as we carefully stepped over the temple threshold. I stared down at the auspicious board. Because ghosts either travel low to the ground or maybe just shuffle their feet, the raised plank placed at the temple entrance was intentional. It was set to trip the demons from entering. I can testify it didn't work that day.

While Rebecca, our Chinese guide, instructed Mark and me regarding various religious traditions, I noticed a local man following us. With doglike sexual advances, he circled us despite our best maneuvers to lose him in the crowd. Although I didn't have the Mandarin to express my disgust, I decided to rebuke him with a stern American glare instead.

As my eyes met his, our two spiritual realms collided. His eyes spilled over with evil and spun my world from calm Christian into terrified turmoil. Keenly aware that I was grossly unprepared for the situation, I grabbed my husband's arm and sought help from my Chinese Christian friend. As I searched Rebecca's eyes, I realized she was equally unprepared.

Quickly assessing the situation, Mark immediately ushered us back through the entry doors. We briskly exited the temple ground and flagged a cab as the brazen character followed closely behind. As Mark kept the man at bay, Rebecca and I wedged into the taxi and locked the door. Within seconds, Mark slid up front beside the driver and we left the man, who was panting and gyrating in the street.

For the next several months, Mark and I discussed the incident and searched the Scriptures. Jesus and His disciples had encountered these kinds of situations, but had faced them with authority. Where was our lack? How could we live a life of authority?

We discovered an important spiritual principle: authority is given to the submissive.

Because Jesus was subject to the Word, His life carried the weight of the Word. Power of authority comes only through proper submission to authority. Christ's life not only represented God's Word; He personified the Word as well. Jesus submitted to the Word of the Father and therefore had the strength of the Word.

The centurion knew the principle. "For I also am a man under authority, with soldiers under me; and I say to this one, 'Go!' and he goes, and to another, 'Come!' and he comes" (Matt. 8:9). This soldier was first a man under authority, and then led others powerfully because of his proper alignment. His word carried authority because he knew obedience.

Some of my best childhood memories on the farm included accompanying my dad to the cotton field. "Two in and two out," he planted two single elevated rows of cotton next to two ground level rows used for carrying water. Though time-consuming, this process of irrigation produced better cotton.

Along the edges of the irrigated land ran a deep ditch, pumped full of water from our well. The water flowed onto the cotton rows through curved metal pipes, which my dad would move from a saturated row to a dry one every few hours. To begin the flow through the pipes, he rhythmically scooped water into one end of the pipe, while creating suction on the other. Within seconds, water was flowing upward through the pipe. It traveled up over the edge of the ditch and back down through the other end of the pipe onto the row of cotton. My dad kept the irrigation pipes free from sand, mud, and debris, because a blocked pipe carried less water.

Our lives reflect the action of the irrigation tube as we allow God's power to pass through us into the lives of others. To the extent that you are open to His control, you outsource His blessing. It is His desire to flow living water through you (John 7:38).

The Lord has given you His authority. Released to influence others, His authority is strengthened to the extent that we align underneath Him. As Christ washes rebellion from you, His power flows outward to melt the rebellion in those for whom you pray. Allowing Him to flow through you empowers your requests to flow to others.

In the parable of the homebuilders, Jesus spoke of two kinds of men: one who heard the Word and obeyed—another who heard and walked away. Both men experienced the inevitable storms of life, but only one man survived. Jesus delivered this story with surprising command because His life was unique among the leaders of the day. He was properly aligned to the Father. The masses recognized Jesus' authority because His life was one of hearing and obeying. He not only heard the voice of the Father, but He also lived out that which He heard (Matt. 7:24–29).

As you subject yourself to Christ's authority, you become the conduit for His life to others. Your mouth can only speak irrefutably about that which you are currently yielding to Him. If you want to pray for someone else who lies, make sure you are also yielding Him areas of deception in your own life. Powerful prayer is a result of powerful submission.

Think of the times that you have cried out on behalf of someone else, but have seen absolutely no change within that person's heart. Could it be that you are asking the Lord to change his or her heart without being willing for Him to transform your own? Often the Lord allows us to recognize deep needs in our loved ones so that He can first begin His work within us.

When a servant submissive to Him speaks His Word, the authority of the living Word comes through. Jesus' lived out what He said because He was the very embodiment of the Word. His words were His actions. His words were an overflow of a life submitted. Authority comes from having already relinquished what you ask others to do.

For whom do you currently carry the greatest burden? Why? Now take a moment to ask the Lord to reveal any area of your flesh that reflects that same fault. (Realize that you may have buried this attitude so deeply that it may take days for you to see it clearly.) Next time, before whining to the Lord regarding the sin of another, commit to placing your own disobedience into His hand first. Then, stand back and watch His power flow out toward the both of you.

Holy Father,

I confess to You today my nit-picking. I spend far too much time needling at the speck in someone else's eye, when my own is blocked with something far larger (Matt. 7:3–4). I see now why my words have no power. I know more than I obey. Please realign me with Your will.

You have revealed truth to me in this matter and I tremble knowing how much ground I've given this attitude of the flesh. Because I desire to live a life of strength, I will submit daily to Your authority. It is only as I am weakened that You are strengthened (2 Cor. 12:10). Decrease my fleshliness so that Your Spirit may increase (John 3:30). May my gentlest whisper hold the utterance of Your power (1 Pet. 4:11). Because of Your name, I pray, Amen.

CHAPTER 10

THE SOUL AND THE WORD

Bible Reading: Matthew 10–12

> "He who has found his life [literally: soul] will lose it and he who has lost his life [soul] for My sake will find it" (Matt. 10:39).

I function by remote control. You see, I have a pulsating electrical device implanted into my hip to manage chronic back pain. Two flat paddles are imbedded onto either side of my spinal cord and together, they send electronic impulses to the nerve center of my brain. The idea is that the electric sensation will scramble the feeling of pain before my brain realizes that I am hurting.

My daughters were teenagers when I had the dorsal column stimulator surgically implanted. You can imagine the ribbing they gave me about carrying a remote control in my purse. They had images of being able to turn up my impulse from across the room and watch me dance. Thankfully, the device only responds when the remote makes contact with the battery. Hallelujah for the small things!

The Word has also been implanted into the spirit of every believer (James 1:21). Our empty spirit came to life with activity the day

His Spirit entered in (1 Cor. 3:16). Now, He has set up our spirit as the communication hub for all spiritual information (Rom. 8:16).

Unlike our flesh, our spirit has the capacity to see the unseen and invisible (2 Cor. 4:18). Despite what we say or do in the flesh, deep within every Christian is a place that is actually delighting to do the will of God (Ps. 40:8). Within our spirit, we agree with the angels and remain peacefully settled in believing the Word (Ps. 119:89). In that inner temple of the spirit, we are actually glorifying Him on automatic pilot (Ps. 29:9)! Isn't that encouraging?

With my stimulator implant, my brain can either receive impulses from pain sensors or from the embedded electrodes. In somewhat the same way, our soul can react either to spiritual signals or to fleshly urges. Situated between the spirit and the flesh, our soul can go either way with thoughts, feelings, and affections.

Before salvation, our soul has only one option: to live by the dictation of the flesh. Without the life of Christ within our heart, the soul is impenetrably veiled. Like the heavy veil of the tabernacle separating the inner court from the Holy of Holies, the unregenerate soul is veiled away from the spirit, thus prohibiting consistent Spirit-influence over our thoughts and feelings (Exod. 26:31–33).

However, when our Messiah yielded up His own Spirit at death, the veil of Herod's temple was not the only veil ripped from top to bottom (Matt. 27:50–51). The shroud between soul and spirit split open as well (Heb. 10:20). When we believe, God's Holy Spirit so greatly energizes our spirit that the fullness spills over into our souls as well. That's the reason that often a new decision for Christ comes with tears of joy. Our personality now has the alternative of operating from the Spirit's perspective (Heb. 10:19–22). Because His love gushes from His Spirit into our hearts, we can also choose to allow His overflow to stream into our innermost being (Rom. 5:5; John 7:38).

The problem is that as long as we remain on earth, our soul continues to makes choices. Throbbing with personality, our soul may submit to the Spirit's direction as we are confronted with His Word, or turn to follow the flesh at the first sign of difficulty. We can either lose our soul to the flesh or find our soul's fulfillment through the Spirit (Matt. 10:39).

The apostle Paul knew the same struggle. He confessed to obeying the Spirit in his inner man, while at the same time his flesh was waging war in his soul against the Spirit (Rom. 7:22–23). You see, the seat of our affection is influenced by whatever attracts our attention (Rom. 8:5–6).

Picture yourself on a dark night at the summit of a mountain. Beside you is a large telescope. As you peer through it, the starry skies are opened to you as never before. Pinpoints of light become brilliant luminaries as you see them enlarged through the refraction of the telescope lens.

Stationed within the center of the soul is an invisible telescope called the will. Every choice ever made first passes through this device before initiating action. Designed to swivel, this single-minded spyglass is the sole courier of information to the soul. All influence of thought and emotion travels through its lens. If we fix our eyes upon criticism, our emotions receive those words inside and react accordingly. Shift the scope just a bit, and new data spills onto the old, creating a new variation of the same disposition.

As long as our hands are on this inner telescope, our personalities will bear the direct influence of the flesh. At best, our most diligent search for good can only yield some form of religion. Although a shadow of Christ, religion itself can never make us better (Rom. 3:20). Many Christians spend years adjusting their telescopic focus one degree or another, but in the end, religion just becomes their new law. No one is justified by the law, whatever it is (Gal. 3:11). No matter what efforts we make, our manipulations can never focus on the Spirit.

The good news is that there is a hidden lever. Lift your hand off the telescope just a moment and you will discover a small toggle switch within your will. The Father placed it at your fingertips because He knew that you needed another option. Snap it from "manual" to "automatic" and take your hands off the telescope.

Everything within you may scream against this action, but doing so actually releases control of your will to the Holy Spirit. Realize that you aren't the self in self-control. When you control self, self-control is actually very limited. Self-control is a fruit of the Holy Spirit. He is the "self" in the control (Gal. 5:23).

Trust Him as the creator of your inner will. This hands-off approach allows Him to calibrate your perspective gradually to a dimension rarely seen. The automatic mode magnetically aligns our perspective to Christ, the Word.

Herein lies the secret of knowing Christ (Phil. 3:10). He takes that which is seen in the heavenlies and discloses His glory into us (John 16:14). This hands-off living allows Him to guide us into all truth (John 16:13). How awesome is our God!

Of course, allowing the Holy Spirit influence over our thoughts and emotions also means declaring war with our flesh (2 Cor. 10:3-5). Never underestimate the hostility that your fleshly nature has toward God's Spirit (Rom. 8:7; Gal. 5:17). Often the flesh literally pushes the reigns of the will back into our hands. Even after releasing all authority into the hands of Christ, we may find ourselves doing the very thing we swore we'd never do (Rom. 7:19–20).

So what hope is there for our success? Consider Paul's own testimony: "Not that I have already obtained it or have already become perfect, but I press on" (Phil. 3:12). Even after numerous miracles and missionary journeys, Paul himself admits his lack of perfection. The secret then is not perfection in hand's-off living.

No, our phenomenal freedom lies in Christ's ongoing forgiveness without condemnation. Let me repeat this astonishing fact: God's Spirit has entered into our spirits despite the fact that He knows our souls will sometimes revert to a "manual" existence. In spite of this weakness, His forgiveness is all reaching and everlasting. Our ability to stumble is far smaller than His ability to save.

Realize the implant that you've been given. Better than my dorsal column stimulator which merely masks my pain, the living Word has been grafted within you to free your soul from hands-on living (James 1:21). Because the kingdom of God is now within you, you have daily power to let go of your affections and watch the Spirit bring life into real focus within you (Luke 17:21). And when you fail, just remember your Lord, whose lovingkindness is new to you every single day (Lam. 3:20–23).

Holy Father,

Thank You for Your Word, not only in printed form but also, especially, in the form of Your Son (John 1:17). I remain astounded that the very Word that spoke the heavens into existence is the Word that now resides within me (John 1:3; Luke 17:21). As I come before You today, I ask that You, the Word, would spread rapidly within me and be glorified (2 Thess. 3:1). I willingly receive the Word implanted (James 1:21).

It is Your desire that Your children are sanctified completely— body, soul and spirit (1 Thess. 5:23). I ask that You use the sharp edge of Your Word to pierce between my soul and spirit and discern the true source of my thoughts and emotions (Heb. 4:12). May my soul be under the authority of the Spirit, not of the flesh, so that my actions and words would be spiritual as well (Rom. 8:6).

Create in me a longing for the pure milk of the Word, so that the roots of my personality would sprout from deep within Your Spirit. I ask that the seedlings of Your Word grow through my soulish emotions and thoughts, and blossom outward to influence all my actions (1 Pet. 2:2; Luke 11:28). I know that when my spiritual eye is clear, then my whole body will be full of light (Matt. 6:22).

Lord, grant me discernment, so that I can come to recognize the difference between that which is good and which is best. I know this only comes through practice (Heb. 5:14). Teach me how to distance myself from the things that just stir up conflict (1 Pet. 2:11).

I need You to shepherd and guard my soul (1 Pet. 2:25). May I be a contented lamb who fully trusts in her Great Shepherd. I want to know what it means to do all things through Your strength (Phil. 4:13). Restore my soul to be tender and obedient to Your Spirit (Ps. 23:3). In Jesus' name, Amen.

CHAPTER 11

THE ATTRACTION OF THE WORD

Bible Reading: Matthew 13–15

> "And looking up toward heaven, He blessed the food" (Matt. 14:19).

One particular morning, I decided to brave the crowds of Taipei to do a little exploring. My Chinese was still very limited, but I felt sure that I could get downtown. Mark was at work, so I bundled up my preschoolers and flagged a taxi.

By the time the driver arrived at our destination, rush-hour traffic was heavy across all six lanes of Nan Jing East Road. Noticing our chance to cross with the light, I hurried the girls out of the taxi and gave hasty instructions for them to hold hands while I paid the driver.

Glancing at the illuminated crossing signal, I briskly grabbed Hannah's free hand as she clung to her three-year-old sister with the other. We rushed onto the pedestrian crosswalk and Hilary's little legs felt our urgency and ran ahead of my lead.

Out of nowhere, another taxi shot through his red light and onto our zebra-striped crossing. The next thing I knew, Hilary lay sprawled on the street. Scooping her quickly into my arms, the three of us scurried to the median as the traffic light released the next roar of accelerating vehicles.

Shaking miserably, we huddled together on the narrow strip of concrete while gusts from the opposing traffic passing by whipped at our clothes and hearts. As the exhaust filled my lungs, my ears drummed loudly with the sound of my racing heart. Aware of Hilary's soft breathing, I pressed her tightly against my chest and wondered how much blood she was losing. My mind scrambled to think where the closest hospital was, how I would get there, and what I could explain in Mandarin. Five-year-old Hannah clung terrified to my legs.

After ninety of the longest seconds of my life, the light changed again and we made it to the safety of the sidewalk. As I bent down and slid Hilary to my knee, I was shocked to see a very calm, unharmed little girl looking up at me. "Are you okay?" I choked.

I still shiver as I think of her matter-of-fact reply, "Yes, Mommy. The angel pushed the taxi away. Didn't you see him?"

That day, the eyes of my three-year-old peered into a realm that mine did not see. I witnessed a living example of the pure of heart (Matt. 5:8). I'd heard about the Invisible. That day I experienced Him.

In today's segment, Jesus Himself saw something his disciples did not. "And looking up toward heaven, He blessed the food" (Matt. 14:19). Before feeding the five thousand, He peered heavenward to check with the Father on just how to proceed. As one of the pure in heart, He could see God.

We've talked about hearing from the Lord in spirit. Now, let's move on to seeing Him in spirit as well (Job 42:5). "We know that when He appears, we will be like Him, because we will see Him just as He is" (1 John 3:2). That sounds like an event far off in the future, huh? But look at the next verse: "Everyone who has this hope fixed on Him purifies himself, just as He is pure" (1 John 3:3).

As we turn our soulish thoughts upward, looking at Christ cleanses our personalities. Seeing Him is the key for transformation into His image. Granted we will not see His fullness in this life, but every glimpse makes us more like Him (1 John 3:2). The more we focus on Him, the more we are transformed.

In painting a self-portrait, an artist assembles brush, oil, and canvas next to a well-lighted mirror. As he analyses each line and curve of his reflection, he carefully reproduces each contour. The value of the resulting portrait depends not only on his ability to detail but also his ability to express the very spark of his life.

Whether we realize it or not, we are also creating a self-portrait. But when we pick up the brush, we have the option of looking into two very different reflecting glasses. The first is a mirror of our mind, which merely reveals our own self-love. This pseudo-image deceivingly portrays us as more beautiful than we really are. Attracted to our own appearance, we are frustrated to find our brush can never duplicate the image we think we see. Despite endless modifications, our canvas will smear with glaring defects that can never satisfy.

But, there is another mirror. Situated within our spirit, this reflection isn't our own image, but the very radiance of Christ. When He becomes our life, He trades our blemishes for His brilliance (2 Cor. 5:21). Our own reflection vanishes from this mirror, because just as love pushes aside fear, the spirit displaces the flesh (1 John 4:18; 2 Cor. 5:16).

Anyone who watches us paint can soon discover where we have fixed our focus. If we have riveted on Him who is unseen, our priceless masterpiece will come alive with the colors of the His love; if we have absorbed ourselves with our own image, the final value of our portrait is fit only for fire (1 Cor. 3:15).

When we let go of ourselves and illustrate Him, He erupts through us into spontaneous holy action (Ezek. 36:25–27). As Andrew Murray says, "A heart that is filled with the Holy Spirit has access to God and abiding in God's presence is no longer an effort."[2] Christ literally becomes our life (Col. 3:4); not because of something that we do, but because we have stared at His remarkable glory with wide-open eyes.

Throughout your day, quiet your thoughts to turn toward Him. Ask Him to unveil your eyes to see Him as He is. Remember not to dwell upon your inability and restlessness, but on Him. After all, it's not about you, it's about Him.

Holy Father,

How can I spend so much time looking at my own reflection? What a waste of time. I ask that You forgive me for my self-absorption and egocentric viewpoint. I need help.

Turn my perspective toward Your Face. Reveal Your brilliance that I may stare with wide-open eyes as I am mesmerized at Your radiance (Ezek. 1:28). You are truly remarkable—a baffling likeness into which I am being transformed.

At first, the glimpse of Your glory seems distant and difficult to distinguish. I guess my spiritual pupils aren't accustomed to this much illumination. But as I continue to allow Your magnetism to draw my attention, I find myself entering into Your glory, overtaken with Your beauty as You engulf me (John 6:44; 2 Cor. 3:18). I desire to walk in the scope of Your splendor. Give me the faith to turn away from my flesh, and run with abandon into Your marvelous Light (Acts 13:39; 1 Pet. 2:9).

Selah. What else can I say?

---

2   Andrew Murray, *The Spiritual Life* (New Kensington, PA: Whitaker House, 1996), 71.

CHAPTER 12

THE PROVISION OF THE WORD

Bible Reading: Matthew 16–19

> "I will give you the keys of the kingdom of
> heaven; and whatever you bind on earth shall
> have been bound in heaven, and whatever you
> loose on earth shall have been loosed in heaven ...
> Again, I say to you, that if two of you agree on
> earth about anything that they may ask, it shall
> be done for them by My Father who is in heaven"
> (Matt. 16:19; 18:19).

After a short ride on the elevator, I took out the borrowed key
and unlocked the red metal door. I had visited my neighbor's
Taiwan apartment before, but this was my first time to disarm
Mrs. Wang's security and enter on my own. Leaving my shoes
outside, I slid into the red leather slippers and stepped onto the
cool tile floor. Mei's family was in Japan on vacation and I'd been
asked to feed their tropical fish.

Mei's apartment had the same square footage as ours, but glancing
around reminded me that the similarities ended there.

Passing the 100-gallon saltwater aquarium, I peered again into
her fully equipped Karaoke room. Built-in seating gathered

comfortably around a glass tapas and wine table. Microphones lay idle in front of the forty-two inch flat screen, as if poised for the next party.

Sliding open paperlike *shoji* doors, I stepped up into the Japanese style tearoom. The aromatic scent of chrysanthemum tea lingered in the air. Coral floor pillows caught my eye and I imagined guests seated cross-legged beside the low *kotatsu* table. The raised tatami floor was slick beneath my slippers and I steadied myself before carefully approaching her limited-edition porcelain collection. With hands in my pockets, my eyes touched the exquisite Lladró pieces, turning them over and again in my mind.

As I returned to the fish, I felt the key to her apartment inside my pocket. I knew it looked just like mine. Then, I smirked a little. There was one obvious difference. Her key held a lot more value than mine.

You too have access to an amazing key. Connecting you directly to the heavenlies, your key carries far more than mere wealth. Your spiritual key gives you Kingdom authority.

During the time of Christ, the terms *binding* and *loosing* were well-known idioms. Any Jew on the street would know that these two words simply meant to prohibit or allow. One teacher of the law might *bind* a certain action on the Sabbath, while another would freely *loose* the same behavior.

Jesus used these everyday words in reference to spiritual locking and unlocking. Our English version "shall have been loosed in heaven" doesn't clearly explain the depths of His thoughts. Using the perfect tense of the verb, Christ emphasized that the action on His part was a once and done accomplishment. Whatever was permitted in heaven was an undertaking that had already been loosed long ago.

The Creator of both the lock and the key doesn't have to try again and again to gain access. When He speaks His permission, the way is automatically opened up. The key of His Word works immediately and remains unchanged.

Before we were ever given the key, the Father was busy opening doors to the heavenly storehouses. In order to make sure all was readied for His children, God prepared what we would need for life and godliness. Glimpse into the unseen with me to see that which stands wide-open for us. Make sure you read the references! These are amazing.

The following are ready for pickup in the heavenlies:

- A gushing of God's love into your heart: Romans 5:5
- Release from legalistic living: Romans 7:6
- Most holy status for His believers: 1 Corinthians 1:2
- A life of good works—already prepared for us in the Spirit: Ephesians 2:10
- God's approval: Ephesians 4:7
- The beginning and completion of your holiness: Philippians 1:6; Colossians 2:10
- Righteousness: Philippians 1:11

Now, like the safety deposit box at our local bank, opening the heavenly storehouse requires two keys: His and our own. Although God's action of binding and loosing is already completed, the vast resources won't reach us without us turning our keys as well.

I heard that little voice that just went off in your head. I had one, too. "I knew there was a catch. I'm the one who always fumbles everything I touch. I'm sure I couldn't truly be entrusted with such a key. All of the resources couldn't possibly be for me."

That's okay. The Father knew we would doubt His lavishness. In fact, Jesus expressed this very thought as He explained how we would handle keys of the kingdom.

Go back to Matthew 16:19. Check out that word "whatever." Did you realize that the original Greek actually means "if" or "in case"? *2 will give you the keys*

*"In case you ever loose anything on earth, know that it will already have been permitted in heaven."

eye felt

Owning the key grants you an option. "In case you want to use this key," Jesus says, "Here it is. I've already taken care of things on my end." We may choose when or even if we'll use the key.

Let's go back up to those resources already available in heaven. I'm going to choose the one that is hardest for me to grasp—the fact that I am truly righteous. Now, let's insert it into our new understanding of Kingdom authority.

Christ has already opened the door that we may be righteous. Jeremiah and Zacharias prophesied it before Jesus' birth (Jer. 23:6; Luke 1:74–75). Paul and Peter testified of it after the Lord's resurrection (2 Cor. 5:21; 1 Pet. 2:24). The delivery door for our righteousness has been standing open for quite some time.

In our hand, we hold the other key. At whatever point we decide by faith to loose His righteousness into our lives, the transaction is ready for relocation. Christ has authorized the release of these resources, in case we ever get the courage to receive them.

Whether the timing of our faith is in past, present, or future tense doesn't change His intended outcome. In fact, the gift is so large that delivery usually necessitates several installments. Yet, time doesn't affect the certainty of the treasure. Faith is your key.

Don't you see? Everything you currently need is already packed up and waiting for you. Christ has done His part and even given you the key to the passageway. Faithe Him and watch all this and more literally spill abundantly within you.

So what about the binding? Which items are already forbidden in heaven? Check out what God has locked away for your good:

- Slavery to sin: Romans 6:6
- His condemnation: Romans 8:1
- His discrimination: Acts 15:9
- His partiality: Romans 2:11
- Temptation that we just can't escape: 1 Corinthians 10:13

As "frail creatures of dust," the Spirit and the flesh continue the war for our soul. Since Christ Himself knew the earthly need to continually entrust Himself to the Father, He gave us permission to grasp it gradually as well. He has pulled off us the pressure of the deadline. The work that He has completed in the heavenlies awaits our timing to actualize it.

The keys of the kingdom are not for you alone, but for all His heirs. While we are unlocking His treasures, others are also trying out their keys as well. When we come together as the body, our power to bind and loose multiplies.

Our collective prayer power is like the oversized dumping bucket at the Kaohsiung Water Park. Elevated above the fountains and forts, this 250-gallon pail hangs just off-center, above the wading pool. Fed with trickles of water through two bright red pipes, the bucket suspends precariously over its next target. When enough water is pumped inside, the container reaches its tipping point and dumps cool refreshment to whomever waits underneath.

Our individual prayer may seem only a drop in the bucket toward addressing problems. Yet, join two or three believers together for intercession and the flow increases. What seems like a trickle of blessing when we pray alone will build into a flood as we collectively join. On occasion, concerted prayer has been offered on my behalf and I've been the one standing underneath the outpouring of His blessings. Talk about needing to hold onto my spiritual swimming suit! United prayer packs a punch.

Spend some time today just waiting underneath the presence of the Father. In silence, be still, meditating on the fact that He is God (Ps. 46:10; Hab. 2:20). As you wait, ask that He show you others with whom you may join in prayer. Once He reveals someone to you, contact him about praying together regularly. When you do meet, use this united time to bind and loose onto earth that which has already been prepared in heaven.

Holy Father, *Christ Jau the way*

Thank You that Your compassion and graciousness far exceeds anything that I have seen here on earth. You are always slow to anger and abound in lovingkindness (Ps. 103:8, 10). Thank You for keeping my frailty in mind when we talk to one another (Ps. 103:14).

I know that You have already prepared good for Your children (Jer. 15:11). It is waiting at the doors of heaven for me to come by and pick up (Jer. 29:11–13). How much more must be waiting that I have yet to discover (1 Cor. 2:9)? Grant me the perseverance to keep on asking, seeking, and knocking with determination and intensity, so that I act like the Kingdom heir that I am (Matt. 7:7–8; Luke 18:2–8).

Right now, my prayers are a mere trickle of what they should be. But I want to wade in and watch You increase them into a river that I can't personally ford (Ezek. 47:1–5). Bring others alongside me in collaborative prayer so that the living flow of blessing would provide an oasis in this dry land. Open up rivers of prayer and springs of intercession in the midst of valleys (Isa. 41:18). Teach us not only to pray, O Lord, but also how to agree with others as we do so. In Jesus' name, Amen.

CHAPTER 13

REQUESTING OF THE WORD

Bible Reading: Matthew 20–22

> "Lord, we want our eyes to be opened"
> (Matt. 20:33).

> "Then He opened their minds to understand"
> (Luke 24:45).

> "And the Lord opened her heart to respond"
> (Acts 16:14).

Why the Lord invites our participation in opening the resources of heaven onto earth remains a mystery. But as so many have said before me, understanding can wait; obedience cannot. Our responsibility is to knock and watch His strength open the gates of heaven through us (Matt. 7:7–8).

開 - "to open"

A good visual for this concept is the traditional Chinese character for "to open." Written with a specific stroke order, there are three main components, each with distinct meaning. Ready for a Chinese lesson?

門 - "door"

The first portion of this script is the pictograph of two ancient doors. Whether a palace or a farmhouse, the Chinese built their structures with only one entrance. It was through these solid wooden doors that access was either granted or blocked.

一 - often means "one"
here represents "bolt"

Attached on the interior of each door was a hewn wooden hook. When the doors were closed, these two pegs served as a resting place for a large beam. In place, this log effectively fastened the doors from the inside. With a simple straight line, our symbolized character depicts this bolt, written horizontally from left to right.

廾 - "two hands"

To unbar the door, it took at least two hands, one on either end of the heavy beam. By firmly lifting up the thick six-by-six, both ends of the beam were removed from their fittings so that the doors could be opened.

In His Word, we discover at least three doors that we can knock upon for the Lord to open: eyes to see, minds to understand, and hearts to respond. Each one is specifically mentioned as a part of God's purpose for us. May the Lord unlock His insights as we position our knuckles to knock.

"Lord, open our eyes to see." We've already talked about the importance of seeing Him in order to be transformed. Yet, often our eyes cannot see Truth because they misperceive who He really is. We live in a world that constantly barrages us with misrepresentation of God.

Over time, seeing God from the world's viewpoint is like building a fortress two inches from our nose. As we stare toward Him, we won't really see Him at all; just our tower of speculation about

[handwritten annotations: 2 Cor 4:5 / weapons to destroy / Have divine pwr. / To destroy strongholds / we destroy / argue / nasty + every / proud / obliere to knowl.dge / of God + take thought / captive to / obey / Christ]

Him. Paul encourages us to break down this stronghold of deceit and bring every thought to Christ to mortar into place (2 Cor. 10:4–5). By doing so, we are asking that He open our eyes to see, thereby releasing His worldview into our souls.

"Lord, open our minds to understand." Imagine the disciples huddled together after Christ's death. His sudden materialization frightens them deeply, for they had just watched Him die (Luke 24:37). As their fear turns to astonishment, He opens their minds to understand how He was their Resurrection as well as their Life (Luke 24:45; John 14:6). Only then could their minds understand how the Living Word in their midst related to the Torah that they had memorized as boys.

Just as the resurrected Christ opened the minds of His disciples, He stands ready to loose our minds to understand Truth. Despite the fact that His thoughts remain infinitely higher than our own, it is His desire to freely reveal to us His wisdom (Isa. 55:9; Matt. 11:25). And just like the disciples, unbelief will be our greatest blinder to His truth (2 Cor. 4:4). Yet, when we give Him the key to our minds, He will open unto us His very same thoughts (1 Cor. 2:16). *[handwritten: We have the mind of christ]*

"Lord, open our hearts to respond." As a feeler, I find this prayer my most difficult. I desire His work within me, but honestly, there are days that I just don't care enough to reply (Ps. 38:9–10). Not only does my flesh fail, but my heart fails too (Ps. 40:12; 73:26). *[handwritten: my Flesh + my ♡ may fail But God is the strength of my ♡ + my portion forever]*

But there is great news for the emotionally charged. We have One within us who is greater than our variable moods and wavering heart (1 John 3:20)! He is even greater than our willpower or personal zeal. When all our vows of commitment fail, our spirit accommodates a Strong Rock that cannot be unsettled. There is no earthquake of emotion, thought, or word that can shake Him out of our hearts. Hannah Whitall Smith said it best: "It is your purpose God looks at, not your feelings about that purpose.

And your purpose or will is therefore the only thing you need to consider."

As the Lord allows us a glimpse into the spiritual concept of "loosing," we are astounded to realize the vast resources that are just awaiting our pickup. Remember, the Lord stands ready with His key. He is just waiting for us to show up with ours.

Holy Father,

I am truly baffled why You would give me the keys of the Kingdom (Matt. 16:16–19). I stand here at the threshold realizing that just one day here is better than years anywhere else (Ps. 84:10). Allow me to catch a glimpse of Your beauty as You beckon me in (Ps. 27:4).

I've come today with several requests signed by Your Son. I join with Him in asking that You open my eyes to any blind spots in my life. I realize that in requesting this, I'm also asking that You reveal ways that I walk in the flesh, so that I may turn to walk in Your truth (John 3:21). So go ahead, Father, open my eyes.

I also ask that You open my mind to understand Your Word (Luke 24:45). I realize that there is a great deal of renewing that needs to take place in my thoughts, but with Your guidance I'm ready to take the necessary steps (Rom. 12:2). I'm warning You that my mind is often scattered, but I'll cast that anxiety Your way and let You worry about that (1 Pet. 5:7).

My last request is that You open my heart to respond to You (Acts 16:14). I confess that sometimes I don't really feel obedient, so I ask in advance that You make me willing to be willing. Let me see just how much bigger You are than my shifting emotions and grant me the motivation to respond.

Signed by Jesus' name, Amen.

willing to be willing grant me motivation to respond — look at Christ not ME

CHAPTER 14

ENDURANCE AND THE WORD

Bible Reading: Matthew 23–25

> "The one who endures to the end, he will be saved" (Matt. 24:13).

Although we knew it to be typhoon season, we chose to fly to Taipei anyway. Mark, my personal meteorologist, warned me to expect turbulence on the thirty-minute flight, so together we decided to forego breakfast. Without the convenience of a covered jet-bridge, we forded the drenched tarmac and boarded the plane in a soaking rain.

Most of our fellow passengers seemed unconcerned about the weather and brought their breakfast along for the short haul. The smells of fried pork, steamed cabbage, and pickled mustard leaves permeated the air as the seasoned travelers devoured their *baozi* and *fan tuans*. As if on cue, the regular commuters finished the last bite as the flight attendant strapped in for takeoff.

Our small turbo-prop made a valiant effort to go around the brewing storm, but let's just say that no one got out of their seats on that flight—at least not intentionally. Like a world-class bull rider, our twin engine bounced and pitched through the air while most of the food that had just gone down came back up. The airsick bags not in use were all near at hand.

If the smells and motion weren't bad enough, the sounds of gagging and heaving made it difficult not to join in. I have never spoken so directly and firmly to my abdomen as I did that day. It was a wrestling match, but in the end, I endured the turbulence and gained mastery over my wavering stomach. A little over an hour after takeoff, Mark and I staggered down the stair ramp and onto stable ground.

There are some situations in life where endurance is the only option. The circumstances may not have been your choice and were certainly not your preference. But you discover that nothing seems to make a difference. In those times, the only change that takes place is within you when you choose to endure.

Endurance is a choice (Heb. 11:25). I've found personal passion expendable and mine has worn thin over time. Often, withstanding an insurmountable crisis is easier than trudging through the tedious and mundane. In fact, the mere unknown of a situation often proves more intolerable than the circumstances themselves.

Yet, "you have need of endurance" (Heb. 10:36). Why is that?

For one thing, it's through endurance that we are able to receive our inheritance. We are all about loosing His blessings out of heaven, but do we realize that only through endurance can we procure the promises (Heb. 10:36)? "If we endure, then we shall reign with Him" (2 Tim. 2:12).

Endurance not only pleases the Father but is actually good for us as well, because it grants us discipline (1 Pet. 2:20; Heb. 12:7). Whether we realize it or not, we have probably asked to be disciplined. If we have prayed for any form of holiness, then we have effectively asked the Lord to work endurance in our life. Those annoying people or situations that keep cropping up are just answers to our prayers. "He disciplines us for our good, so that we may share His holiness" (Heb. 12:10).

The best part of endurance is the effect it has upon our wavering soul. We remain daily aware of the war that flesh wages within our personality. Some days, we find that we serve the Lord from our spirit and other days our flesh has the victory. It's a continual struggle. *battle*

But we are told that it is by endurance that we can "gain" our souls (Luke 21:19). The literal Greek interpretation of this last phrase means, "to acquire the true life your souls[3]." Buckling down to withstand proves the best remedy for our indecisive souls. Endurance captures our vacillating personality and holds it under the authority of the Spirit.

Sure, endurance holds great promise for the future. But how do you get through it in the meantime? Ask the Spirit if any of these suggestions could be useful while you endure:

1. Start the morning with a prayer, submitting the day to Him (Prov. 16:3). Ask to see life through His eyes.
2. Focus on one day at a time (Matt. 6:34). See bedtime as your finish line, not years down the road. *Present yourself to*
3. Do a topical study (2 Tim. 2:15). Research the themes of *God* worry or anxiety. Rather than reading someone else's writings *as 1* on the subject, go directly to the Word. Use a concordance to *approved* look up biblical references on the topic, then cross-reference *no need* verses that stand out to you. *Strong's Exhaustive Concordance, Nave's* *to be* *Topical Bible,* and *The Treasure of Scriptural Knowledge*[4] are three *ashamed* good launching pads. You can find these in the library as well as *Rightly* online. Note that the evil one will tempt you to adopt a "holier *the* than thou" attitude in studying only the Word. Resist him and *Word of* *Truth*

---

3 Joseph Thayer, *Thayer's Greek-English Lexicon of the New Testament* (Peabody, MA: Hendrickson, 1996), s.v. "Luke 21:19."

4 All three of these resources and more are found by searching the verse on www.blueletter.com.

he will flee from you (1 Pet. 5:9). Your study is to glorify God, not gain knowledge.

4. Read a chapter of Proverbs every day for a month or so.

Proactively plan small celebrations in your month, week, and day. They could be weekly picnics in the park or relaxing and listening to your favorite music. Give yourself something to look forward to that is well within your budget and energy.

5. Find someone to talk to about your situation (Eccles. 4:9–10). Choose someone who already knows you well and knows the Word well. If you have to choose between these two qualities, choose the latter over the former. Keep the conversation focused on Christ, not your situation.

6. Don't talk about your situation to everyone. Often, you will hear more discouraging things than you bargain for.

7. Laugh (Prov. 17:22; Eccles. 2:25). Reminisce about times that brought you joy. Watch a classic comedy or a clean comedian.

8. Don't neglect your appearance (Matt. 6:16–18). Although this principle speaks of fasting, it can be applied to times of endurance as well.

9. Be especially cautious about high fat and binge eating (Dan. 1:8–19). This is unhealthy and causes your soul to unnecessarily pity your body.

10. Walk more. This helps your circulation and actually increases your endurance in the long run.

I've saved the best for last. Endurance is one of the many attributes of love (1 Cor. 13:7). Learning this discipline actually increases our capacity to love and know love. If we desire to love deeply, then we must press through to experience its every quality, even endurance. May the Lord grant you endurance from His Spirit as you walk through today.

Holy Father,

Although endurance is a part of Your character, I have to admit that it still doesn't make surviving it any easier. I do appreciate You giving so many examples of perseverance in the Word because *whatever is written was for our instruction — by steadfastness we may have hope by encouragement*

it gives me hope to realize that others have accomplished the same things that I am experiencing (Rom. 15:4). Thank You not only for granting me a spirit to endure but also for giving me encouragement (Rom. 15:5). I really need Your renewal to get through this time.

Thank You Jesus for all You endured on my behalf. It means so much to know that although You didn't have to, You gave up equality with God to become like me (Phil. 2:6–7). When I sob, You can relate as Your prayers included loud crying with tears just like mine (Heb. 5:7). Endurance becomes a little easier when I see that You had to learn it as well (Heb. 5:8).

Strengthen me with Your power, so that I can attain steadfastness with joy (Col. 1:11). I need You to sanctify me entirely, spirit, soul, and body so that I can be found faithful (1 Thess. 5:23). I won't be able to finish strong if I don't have Your Presence (Exod. 33:15). Show me Your glory (Exod. 33:18). In Jesus' name, Amen.

Strengthen me FATHER as I stand comfort me when sorrowful, and lead me 2 everlasting life. help me 2 stand firmly on the promise of life everlasting.

CHAPTER 15

THE FLESH VERSUS THE WORD

Bible Reading: Matthew 26–28

> "The spirit is willing, but the flesh is weak" (Matthew 26:41).

Endurance sure has a way of exposing our weakness, doesn't it? When we are called to persevere, we soon run out of our own energy and scramble to draw energy from any source readily available. Unfortunately, the soul usually turns to anything convenient to get through stressful situations. And in my case, that is often the flesh.

Of course, Jesus too knew of endurance. In the midst of His own persistent battle, He spoke clearly to Peter of the trial to come. Peter, like Christ, would have two options: a willing spirit or a weak flesh (Matt. 26:41). Christ remained plugged into the Spirit. Peter, however, defaulted to his anemic flesh (Matt. 26:69–75).

What then are the qualities of this flesh? Why does it cause so much trouble? Let's check out qualities of the flesh:

- The flesh is full of jealous rivalry and contention (1 Cor. 3:3). *of flesh jealousy + envy*
- The flesh always fails when it tries to do something for God (Rom. 7:15–23). *I DO that which I would not + do not that which I* 66 *would no* *better in me*

- The flesh is self-absorbed and can never arouse anything spiritual within us (John 3:6; Rom. 8:6).
- The flesh can never praise God because it cannot stand to be in His Presence (1 Cor. 1:29).
- Religion can't clean up the flesh. (Rom. 3:20; Gal. 2:16).
- Flesh never reveals spiritual information and cannot inherit the Kingdom of God. (Matt. 16:17; 1 Cor. 15:50).
- The flesh is of no use to God, because it never pleases Him (John 6:63; Rom. 8:8).

That's a pretty hopeless list, huh? Yet, our soul defaults to our flesh day after day. No wonder we remain distracted and restless. We have been made right with God in spirit, but as long as we default to the flesh, we aren't going to feel that way.

One of my early journal entries gives hint to the struggle:

"Lord, flesh is like the musty attic to my soul. Whenever I crack the door, I find selfishness and arrogance seem to have an evil dice game going. Sin, the master from which I have died and been set free, still hovers around in my flesh, trying to entrap me away from living like the Kingdom child that I have become (Rom. 6:10–11; 7:17).

Oddly enough, my soul sometimes sneaks up the steps to this cramped enclosure. If I venture there and spend too much time, my eyes become accustomed to the darkness and I resort to choosing the flesh over Your Spirit. You said that flesh is weak, but I sure spend a lot of energy on it (Matt. 26:41).

Enticingly, sin disguises itself in garments of outward beauty. His silken words twist my desire for truth and invite me to try on old garments of self-abasing religion. These appear elegant and dignified, but are weighty and restrictive upon my shoulders (Col. 2:23). Remind me daily who I am and to whom I belong."

Can you relate?

Well, you aren't alone. Unfortunately, most Christians live this attic existence. One moment, we are seeking to peer into the heavenlies and the next moment we are sneaking into the attic of the flesh. We think that this counts as "higher living", but in reality it's just the same old residence. Allowing the soul a freedom of choice makes it all too easy to slip back into old thought patterns.

So how can we keep the attic door closed away from our fleshly lifestyle? Actually, this is the wrong question. The solution does not lie within our ability. You'll be happy to know that the problem has already been dealt with in Christ.

Christ always uses final reality as His frame of reference. When He moved out of His flesh, He took us out of ours as well (Rom. 6:6). And because the soul is so closely linked to the flesh, He has moved us out of both soul and flesh. He didn't just build a new wing onto our soulish residence. Jesus has given us a whole new residence in the spirit (2 Cor. 5:17). The source of our personality has been moved inside of Christ (Col. 3:3). It's a done deal. It's already happened. *if we in christ we R A new creation*

With this in mind, we are no longer confined within the housing of soul and flesh, but may step afresh into the wide-open spaces of the spirit. Here, in this spiritual garden, Eden is restored that we may walk at peace with God (Rom. 5:1). He has made us one spirit with Him, and he desires that we walk broadly in the expanse of His freedom (1 Cor. 6:17; Gal. 1:5). In the spirit, He draws us after Him that we may run together with rejoicing (Song of Sol. 1:4). It's like moving from a cramped prison cell into owning a vast and magnificent kingdom. *HE gives power*

There is also rest in this spiritual realm, as He knows our weakness toward fatigue (Isa. 40:30). He provides us with the shade of His Presence and invites us to delight in the fruit of His Word as we commune with Him (Song of Sol. 2:3). The fruit of the tree of

As an apple Tree so is my beloved with buds I sit in His shadow, His Fruit sweet to my taste

[handwritten notes in top margin: "showed me river of waters of life and tree of life with 12 fruit"]

life not only heals us but also sprouts forth love, patience, and self-control that everyone can see (Rev. 22:2; Gal. 5:22–23).

Since we know this, our only response is to consider it true. "Knowing this, that our old self was crucified with Him ... even so consider yourselves to be dead to sin, but alive to God in Christ Jesus" (Rom. 6:6,11). Paul had to remind himself of this fact daily (1 Cor. 15:31). We should do the same. Your residence has changed. Are you living like it?

Holy Father, *[handwritten note: "many rooms I go to prepare a place 4:4."]*

Thank You for preparing a place for me to be where You are (John 14:2). Even before the foundation of the world, You desired that all who believe in You would behold Your glory (John 17:24). It's awesome to realize that includes me.

By sending Your Son to exchange His life for mine, You have effectively moved the core of my personality from the flesh to the spirit (Rom. 8:9). Sharpen my spiritual eyes to see the realm of the heavenlies that You have prepared for me. Anchor my soul to life sourced beyond the veil and into Your Spirit (Heb. 6:19). Give me the daily encouragement that I need to stay in Your refuge of hope (Heb. 6:18).

Of course, as long as my body lives, I will continually have to entrust my life to You. I'm encouraged as I remember that even Jesus did that while He was in the flesh (1 Pet. 2:23). But, the final reality remains: sin was once and for all dealt with by Your sacrifice (Heb. 10:26). Hallelujah that the outcome is secured despite the numerous times that I fail.

Grant Your people the insight to live in the wide-open spaces of Your Kingdom, even if it means having to endure ill-treatment here on this earth (Heb. 11:25). May we see past the physical and into the spiritual where our true reward lies (Heb. 11:26). Show us the unseen in order that we may endure (Heb. 11:27). In Jesus' name, Amen.

CHAPTER 16

THE POWER OF THE WORD

Bible Reading: Mark 1–4

> "But no one can enter the strong man's house and plunder his property unless he first binds the strong man, and then he will plunder his house" (Mark 3:27).

> "When a strong man, fully armed, guards his own house, his possessions are undisturbed. But when someone stronger than he attacks him and overpowers him, he takes away from him all his armor on which he had relied and distributes his plunder" (Luke 11:21–22).

Remember my clash with the demon-possessed man? Well, what I had thought to be a cultural awareness outing turned out to be a defining point in my life. Not only had I witnessed sacrifices and worship to a plethora of unholy gods, but my spiritual clash in the temple that day also jarred my reality. My American theology had no answer for the conflict of spirits that had been so real. Caught off-guard, I worried that the spirit of darkness might be more powerful than my weak faith. With increasing intensity, I turned my focus from Love to fear.

Like the flame of a single match in a forest without rain, fear ignited my thoughts and emotions. I stayed within our apartment more and more as I dreaded stepping out onto the streets. Panic attacks crippled my language study and confused my ability to plan a meal. As repressed fears from childhood resurfaced, I retreated from reality. Mark's prayers turned to desperate cries before the Lord.

One day, upon returning home, Mark found me wedged behind a corner dresser in a fetal position. As he pulled me toward him, he began to claim God's promises over me. Mark kept his eyes open and the Word in his lap as he watched me carefully.

As I heard Truth, the evil one scrambled to stream different thoughts into my mind. Petrified, I choked down with fear. Aware of my stiffening body language, Mark asked, "What are you hearing?"

Hearing only the lies of fear, I was unable to speak. I could almost feel the icy fingers of foreboding clutching my throat. As I began to gasp for air, I clinched my lips in silence.

In all gentleness, I heard Mark say, "In the name of the Lord Jesus Christ, speak what you are hearing."

After another struggle with terror, the inner strength of the Lord allowed me to repeat to Mark what I had been hearing. In weakness and trembling, I whispered, "If I try to assert victory over this, it's just going to return later with seven other feelings that will be worse."

Immediately Mark claimed, "Kandy, this is a word from the evil one. Satan, you are a liar and the father of all lies. You have no authority over Kandy as she is a child of God and possesses the very Spirit of God. In the name of the Lord Jesus Christ, be silenced and leave her alone."

Like a prick to an overextended balloon, the sword of the Word quickly punctured the stronghold of fear, which moments before

71

had loomed so large. I relaxed as peace enveloped me. I knew the immediate release of truth upon my heart. Mark and I sat together, worshipping the Father, who we now knew as our personal Deliverer (Ps. 144:2).

In the days to follow, Mark and I became conscious of the necessity to know the Word. Growing up in America, the ruler of darkness had used every opportunity to misshape subtly our perception of spiritual reality. Like dehydrated individuals requiring emergency IVs, the Word became our super injection of Truth. Mark divided the New Testament into thirty segments and we began reading through its entirety every month. Over the next couple of years, Mark and I went on a literature "fast" in which we read nothing but the Bible and the necessities of Chinese language study.

The passages regarding the strong man began to have special significance. When Christ set up His residence within our spirits, He effectively bound the strong man. But even though we were new creations, we were still living among a corrupted creation. Discovering the authority that Christ already held over our fleshly strongholds was vital to deliverance (Mark 3:27; Luke 11:21–22).

Satan can never "possess" a Christian. The whole gospel message is that our God is "tabernacled" within us. How foolish we are to think that our almighty God would rent out space within us to the evil one!

Yet, Christians can be oppressed in any area that they are unwilling to bring to the Light. In my own life, I had concealed many painful memories. Although I hated most of these attitudes and experiences, the fact that I had buried them granted some strange hold over me.

Curses that were spoken over me as a child were absorbed into my soul and counted as truth. My regression into fear was like slipping upstairs into that secret attic; I was drawn to the mystery but afraid of the revelation. As long as I left them shrouded in shadows, the evil one held influence over those thoughts.

You know, fear is a very, odd strong man. Without the spirits of deceit and despair working alongside him, fear really has no strength within himself. Much like the Wizard of Oz, he works upon us with sleight of hand and lots of noise. Brought into the Light of Love, fear is exposed and powerfully driven away (1 John 4:18).

No matter what you have deep within your memory, remember that these are memories of another person—not you! Even if your guilt stems from actions committed since your faith in Christ, these too have been covered by His blood. As one of His children, you stand forever forgiven by He who is greater than the strong man (1 John 4:4). *HE IN U IS greater than anyone*

In order to realize Jesus' strength on your behalf, bring fear, anger, and guilt into His light. Give Christ those secret thoughts and doubts (Eph. 5:13). Grant Him permission to reframe your mind as you actively turn your thoughts back to His Word (Rom. 12:2; 2 Cor. 10:5). Jesus Himself is praying that you be set apart into truth (John 17:17). Why don't you begin to pray it for yourself? *Thy word is truth*

When Christ overpowered the strong man, He stripped the evil one of his armor and distributed the plunder. Just think: all the hidden images that the evil one once used against you are cleansed by Christ and ready to be used for His glory. This doesn't mean that you must immediately air your story to the public. But as you walk in the light, God will take that which was meant for evil and use it for good (Gen. 50:20). *U meant evil against God but He meant it 4 good 2 bring it about*

Holy Father,

Praise You for being both my Light and my Salvation! Whom shall I fear? You are the defense of my life, even when I am weak. Whom then shall I dread (Ps. 27:1)? You are on my side of the battle! Why then do I worry about those on the other side (Ps. 118:6)? *The LORD is my stronghold*

I confess to You that there are still places in my life I'm not sure I want You to see. But You said that there is nothing covered

[left margin: awake + Christ will give you a light]

[right margin: NOT B do not B conformed 2 this world. But B trans Formed By the renewal of ur mind. you may prove what is will of God]

[right margin: U R strong]

that won't be revealed (Matt. 10:26). I want to ask You to expose anything in me that needs light. I admit that this scares me. But I want to remind You that in doing so, You have to bind the strong man's influence and use all experiences for Your purposes of good (Luke 11:22).

Thank You that I'm free from my past, so that the evil one can't use it against me anymore. Reframe my view of these memories as truly belonging to someone else (Isa. 43:18–19, 25). May the resources of my history now be used to help others escape bondage. Give me complete delivery in Christ.

Teach me to intercede for others dealing with "strong men" in their lives. Clothed with Your armor, I enter the battle on their behalf. I realize that the devil is our adversary and hates all who confess Your name (1 Pet. 5:8). Thank You that I do not have to fear him because You are greater than he is (1 John 4:4). Hallelujah! Just in speaking out this truth, I am overcoming the evil one already by my faith (1 John 5:4). Lord, increase my faith (Luke 17:5). In Jesus' name, Amen.

CHAPTER 17

THE PRAYERS OF THE WORD

Bible Reading: Mark 5–7

> "Immediately Jesus made His disciples get into
> the boat and go ahead of Him ... After bidding
> them farewell; He left for the mountain to pray.
> When it was evening, the [disciples'] boat was
> in the middle of the sea, and He was alone on
> the land. Seeing them straining at the oars ...
> He came to them, walking on the sea; and He
> intended to pass by them" (Mark 6:45–48).

"Peter said to Him, 'Lord, if it is You, command me to come to
You on the water'" (Matt. 14:28).

As I began to heal from my bondage to fear, I expected the
transformation to grant me smooth sailing along the sea of
life. Because truth began to replace memories and anxieties, I
anticipated a tranquil journey ahead. Somewhere along the way,
I had come to expect God's wonderful plan for my life to include
sheer happiness for the obedient.

Why then did I continue in such an emotional cyclone? Why
were my children so rebellious? Why had Alzheimer's taken over
my mother's godly mind?

I found that escaping the kingdom of fear didn't take me out of life on earth. Both the house built on the rock and the one built on the sand experience the tempest (Matt. 7:24–27). Weathering the storm is often when we learn the most. Let's learn from the disciples as we examine today's passage.

What had started as a small group retreat resulted in a mass convention (Mark 6:31, 33). Forced to share their time of solitude with as many as ten thousand, the disciples scrambled to organize while Jesus prepared the meal (Mark 6:44). As the crowd chatted of miracles and monarchy, Jesus' heart returned to the original intent of His day (John 6:15). He sent His disciples on ahead by boat, while He withdrew up the mountain to pray (Mark 6:46).

Jesus' concerns were heavy. He must have thought of His disciples and their great need for unity (John 17:11). He didn't ask that they be taken out of the world, but probably asked that they be kept from the evil one and protected in truth (John 17:15, 17). Whatever His requests to the Father, Jesus remained at this isolated location for several hours in prayer (Mark 6:48).

The cool breeze that swept by Jesus on the mountain, gained momentum as it rushed down the valley to the rocky beach. The once placid waters of the sea foamed and churned as increasing winds whipped across their surface. Although several of the disciples were experienced fishermen, hours after push-off they were still in the middle of the lake, fighting for their life. The storm was so intense that the Greek account says that they were "tortured" with the swell of the waves and in danger of going under (Matt. 14:24).

We do not know if Jesus had a premonition of this storm, but the Gospel of Mark does indicate that Jesus was aware of the disciples' situation. It seems that as He prayed, He could see them "straining at the oars" (Mark 6:48). Can you imagine Him glancing their way as He continued His petitions?

Although Jesus knew their struggle, He did not come to them immediately. Waiting before the Father took precedence. His prayer for them was more important than His actual presence with them. At some point between three and six o'clock in the morning, Jesus heard the Father's release and He immediately set out toward them (Mark 6:48).

It seemed to the disciples that He would pass them by, but indeed this was not the case (refer to Luke 24:28–29). The lake was about eight miles across, but Jesus chose to walk very near their vessel. He easily could have slipped by unnoticed had He chosen to do so. Yet, in spite of the darkness, He maneuvered the wind and waves to the exact spot where each one in the boat could have a full moonlit view of Him.

At first, they thought that He was a ghost from the netherworld signaling their eminent death. But as He spoke over the wind, they recognized His voice. "Take courage; it is I" (Mark 6:50). It was at this point that Peter asked permission to step out of the boat.

In the midst of our own storms, we often wonder if Jesus really cares. Yet, be assured that even while He waits to rescue, His eye is on us. Often His prayers for us are more important than our awareness of where He is. Every minute of our lives He is earnestly discussing our case with the Father (Heb. 7:25). He will never tarry so long that we go under; only long enough for us to become desperate for His Presence.

Are you about to drown in your particular situation? Remember that even if you can't see Him, He can see you. Even now, His gaze in your direction is coupled with specific prayers for your best. No matter how it seems to you, the truth is He is guarding you very carefully (John 17:12).

His arrival is guaranteed, despite any delay. Although His ways and timing are different from our own, He can't help but head straight our way (Isa. 55:9; John 6:19). He will come, and when

He does, we will recognize Him by His voice. Don't let Him pass by without scrambling out of the boat.

Holy Father,

When I look at my future, sometimes the fear of the unknown seems like an approaching storm. Despite my best attempts to outrun the winds of anxiety, I know my sailing experience is inadequate and I find myself caught in the winds of change. Drenched and exhausted, I row on, wondering if You will ever show up.

Thank You for promising that You will never leave me or forsake me (Heb. 13:5). Even now You are not only protecting me and keeping my wavering soul, but Your Son is also praying for me (Ps. 121:7, Rom. 8:34). I couldn't have a better prayer partner!

Strengthen and protect all Your people from the evil one (2 Thess. 3:3). Direct our hearts to love like the Father and remain as steadfast as Christ Himself (2 Thess. 3:5). No matter our circumstance, may we know Your peace, especially amidst situations beyond our control (2 Thess. 3:16). In Jesus' name, Amen.

CHAPTER 18

FAITH IN THE WORD

Bible Reading: Mark 8–10

> "[The father said,] 'If You can do anything, take pity on us and help us!' And Jesus said to him, "'If You can?" All things are possible to him who believes.' Immediately the boy's father cried out and said, 'I do believe; help my unbelief.'" (Mark 9:22–24).

"Mom? Are you awake?"

Hilary's whisper pulled me back into the hospital room and away from the image of her accident. I had dozed off against her bed rail. For the last forty-eight hours, all of my dreams included her lying unconscious on Kenting Road in a pool of her own blood.

"I'm afraid I can't do this," Hilary quivered as she stared up at the ceiling. Immobilized by a neck brace and now traction, her pain medication couldn't keep up with the pain of a cervical fracture. I watched as a tear escaped the corner of her eye and puddled into her ear.

Just yesterday, the China Medical staff had shaved Hilary's temples and inserted two screws on either side of her skull. A U-shaped device was then attached to the screws and a series of weights and pulleys were fastened to reduce pressure to the base of her neck. Paralysis was still a possibility.

As I prayed and sang over Hilary, I too wondered if I would be able to get through the crisis. With my words, I encouraged and comforted. With my thoughts, however, I doubted and feared. My prayers often sounded much like the man in our reading today, "If you can do anything, take pity on us, and help us!"

Months later after a trip back to the United States, Hilary walked through surgical realignment. Dr. Cone reinforced Hilary's neck vertebrae with titanium rods to give her greater neurologic stability. As our family walked through these days, I felt that I had been repositioned as well. The Great Physician strengthened my faith with His Word.

I had always visualized faith as a valuable object to be hoarded. Like an old spinster, I wanted to keep plenty of trust stuffed between my spiritual mattress just in case of need. Because emergencies might demand more than I had accumulated, I dreaded crises with gnawing anxiety.

Yet, the Lord revealed that faith is more like manna than money. Like the coriander wafer given to Israelites each morning, faith is apportioned to us fresh each day (Exod. 16:16; Rom. 12:3). On the days of crisis, our faith fragment is significantly larger than on the days of comfort. It is apportioned to us according to our need. Like manna, we are to use it strongly and fully, to have none left over for the following day. He'll provide for tomorrow just as He provided for today (Matt. 6:34; Ps. 102:27).

Although we realize that we do have faith for salvation, we often fear it will fall short for daily living. Here lies the crux of our problem, for faith is not something we summon, but something God supplies. Faith is a gift whose only benefactor is God (Eph. 2:8). Trust manufactured from good feelings or positive self-thoughts cannot be called faith. If our courage is self-stimulated, it isn't faith at all.

Just because the Father has granted you the gift of faith, doesn't mean that you have activated it. When you request a new Visa card, you must first call the phone number on the sticker before using it. Initiating our faith is much the same. We must take our faith to the Word and allow Him to unite the two together (Heb. 4:2). "So faith comes by hearing, and hearing by the word of Christ" (Rom. 10:17).

If you have a faith problem, it's probably because you are looking in the wrong direction for the solution. It's not within your realm, but within His. Faith is not only a gift from God; it will also grow as you look to Him.

Peel the sticker off today's faith allotment. Together, let's call our Spiritual Banker asking Him to activate our faith. He will speak truth to your heart as you look at Him through His promises.

- I believe that Christ came to do away with sin, I believe that includes mine (1 John 3:5). *u know that HE came 2 take away sins + in Him is no sin*
- I believe that living by a bunch of rules is not the same as living by faith (Gal. 3:12).
- I believe that I am near to God by way of His Spirit inside of me, not because of what I do or don't do (Heb. 7:18–19).
- I believe that even though I often feel inadequate, my adequacy is in God (2 Cor. 3:5). *God can*
- I believe that Christ gives me freedom, not just a different set of rules to keep (Gal. 5:1).
- I believe that since Jesus has given me faith, I don't have to make some type of offering for my sin today (Heb. 10:18).
- I believe that Jesus is praying for me right now (Heb. 7:25).
- I believe that His Spirit desires to speak to me (John 16:13). *When spirit comes HE will guide u into all truth HE will not speak on His own authority but on the authority of Him who sends Him.*

Now it is your turn. Ask Him to guide your mind into promises that you know He has given you. Jot down any portion of the promise you can remember. You can go find its reference later. Allow His truth to refocus your soul. When you come to the end of this time, ask Him to overcome your areas of unbelief. Wait and watch; He loves to answer this prayer. And be greatly encouraged because as you faithe, you are freed (Acts 13:39).

FROM GOD WE are freed from all we could not believe BFREED By the law

Holy Father,

I praise You for never changing (Mal. 3:6). You are the same today as the day I believed in You most (Heb. 13:8). Nothing disturbs You from being constant. Hallelujah.

I earnestly desire to faithe You, but I often find that my prayers begin with the words, "If you can." I know that You have given me a portion of faith, but I admit that I wonder if it is enough. Forgive me for doubting the sufficiency of Your gift.

it is not about me or my faith IT IS ABOUT GOD is any thing too hard 4 God?

I bring the measure of my faith to You, asking that You make it operative through Your Word. Increase my faith in such a way that it can truly shield me from the devil's darts of doubt (Luke 17:5; Eph. 6:16). May I dwell on the power that You have granted me through my faith—the power to overcome the world (1 John 5:4). *born of God overcomes the world*

Thank You for renewing my inner man every single day despite how my body may be aging (2 Cor. 4:16). Give me the insight to walk by faith and not by sight, as I seek resolutely for the things that are not seen by the human eye (2 Cor. 5:7; 2 Cor. 4:18). I believe; help my unbelief (Mark 9:24). In Jesus' name, Amen.

Lk 17:5 if u have faith of a seed you could say Brooted up or planted is rooted up + it would obey u

2 C 4:16 DO NOT lose heart tho our outer nature is wasting away our inner nature is being renewed daily

we walk by faith not sight

2 C 4:18 we look not to those things seen but 2 those things unseen. things seen are transient things unseen are eternal

CHAPTER 19

THE IMAGE OF THE WORD

Bible Reading: Mark 11–13

> "They brought [a denarius]. And He said to them, 'Whose likeness and inscription is this?'" (Mark 12:16).

Have you ever seen an ancient coin underneath the glass of a museum display? Mark and I had the opportunity to do so at the National Archaeological Museum of Athens. As we peered through the glass, we saw that each coin varied slightly from the next as they were forged individually by hand. A far cry from our own industrially minted coins, their imperfections and irregularities just add to their unique antiquity.

When Jesus held up this tribute penny with forefinger and thumb, the Pharisees and Herodians alike knew His question was rhetorical. "Whose likeness and inscription is this?" He had asked. They saw both sides and knew who was on the coin. The imprint had been shaped to look just like the emperor.

In the first-century forging process, heat-softened blanks were inserted between a pair of templates called dies, one of which bore the likeness of Tiberius Caesar. Once positioned upon the anvil, slaves pummeled the sandwich with several blows to imprint the design into the metal. In fact, the very word "likeness" that Jesus used here in Greek means "a die as struck." Tiberius Caesar made sure it was his likeness bludgeoned into each coin.

Jesus' point that day had very little to do with hard, cold cash. He wanted those with ears to listen for the spiritual lesson. He knew that before the need for coins, He was already in existence (John 1:1–2). In fact, He participated in the creation of man, an image formed with the three-dimensional die of body, soul, and spirit (Gen. 1:26).

By God's design, the physical body we were given was not the same as the body of Christ's glory (1 Cor. 15:38; Phil. 3:21). Adam came into the world in the image of his Creator. However, all of Adam's descendants, including you and me, were after Adam's image, born to sin (Gen. 5:1–3). In one generation, all the rest of us were cast into a faint shadow of who man had been created to be (Rom. 5:12).

Like Adam, we came into being as a living soul, but our spirit within was dark, without light or life. Although Adam was breathed into the image of God, the first man's sin assured that you and I would be cast into Adam's fleshly mold. It doesn't matter whether or not we commit the exact sin of the garden, we come into the world "in the likeness of the offense of Adam" (Rom. 5:14).

When Christ asked about the likeness of the coin, He did so to point out the striking difference between the metal image in His hand and the living, breathing Caesar. The original breath of man could only be restored through breaking the old mold and making a brand new one (Luke 5:37–38). The form of legalism had to go.

As you know from experience, keeping rules never results in sustainable closeness to God. That's because this type of spirituality is actually just a modification of the Old Testament model. We'll never please God by what we do (Rom. 3:28). That's the whole reason He gave Moses the law in the first place—to show us how ridiculous it is to think we could follow it. Man had to have another option.

So, unlike the rigid mold that the Law crammed us into, the mold of the Spirit is the very breath of God. Did you realize that what Jehovah breathed into Adam was not just oxygen, but the very Spirit of God (Gen. 2:7)? Just check out the Hebrew translation for that word breath—it can mean either breath or spirit. So, our new life in Christ means we are no longer a lifeless copy of our ancestor Adam, but we are a living, breathing copy of the power of God (2 Cor. 4:7). WE have power in our earthen vessel to show Gods power
While the image on Caesar's coin gradually smoothed away in time, our Master Minter never stops forming us into His likeness (Col. 3:10). Yet His work is from the inside rather than the outside. His Spirit forges us with His love (John 1:13). Our current likeness may be a crude reflection, but one day we will bear the completed image of the heavenly (1 Cor. 13:12; Eph. 4:24; 1 Cor. 15:49).

Like the malleable round of metal between the Roman dies, we are to submit as Christ is formed within us (Gal. 4:19). As we learn of Him, we understand better how He is fashioning us as well. Feel the mighty Hand of His Spirit pulsate deep inside as our pliable souls meld into His image.

Inhale as He impresses upon you how to speak: Jesus never spoke on His own initiative, but only spoke what He heard the Father speaking (John 12:49). We, too, are to have our words sourced from the Spirit and not our own thoughts and emotions. Our words merely repeat what the Father has already said (Matt. 10:20). We don't say what we think. We exhale our Father's words.

Inhale as He impresses upon you how to act: Not only will our mouths be melded with Christ's words, but our actions must follow His example as well. Christ did nothing on His own initiative (John 8:28). His life had power because He always did things "according to the pattern" of the heavenlies (Matt. 6:10).

Because our old mold has been broken, the Spirit's image is now our image. We are brand new (2 Cor. 5:17). His actions spill into us, so we spill out His likeness (John 7:38; 13:15). Since our own actions can never please Him, the law mode has been replaced by the Christ mode (Rom. 3:20: 10:4). Relax into Him and let His Spirit animate you (Heb. 13:20–21).

Exhale your singular response: The only self-initiative that Christ took was to lay down His life (John 10:18). Like Christ did on earth, we have a choice. In order to receive His living imprint upon our hearts, we are to rise up and choose to live for the will of God, not for the desire of the flesh (1 Pet. 4:2).

Because He is Spirit, He will be checking your spirit on this matter, not your flesh. Our Master Blacksmith does not use the iron mallet of the law, but the spiritual breath of faith. Rules and regulations never make anything perfect (Heb. 7:19). When He looks at His workmanship, He critiques according to faith, not according to works (Gal. 2:16). He doesn't need you to do Him favors. He is quite capable of doing the whole work (Isa. 26:12; Ps. 57:2; Phil. 1:6)

Holy Father,

Although You've broken the mold of legalism for me, I'm afraid I've been trying to glue the pieces back together. I did start in the Spirit, but afterward it seems that I've constructed a plethora of regulations so that I can monitor how I am doing (Gal. 3:3). I guess I still have a hard time believing that living in the image of Christ is such a wide, freeing walk.

As I take my hands off trying to please You, come and delight Yourself through me. Breathe Your words and actions through me, so that I might look like the image of Your Son (Rom. 8:29). Give me grace to do my part—that hard part where I don't initiate my own ideas. Thank You for exhaling the image of Your glory into me. May I represent You well. In Jesus' name, Amen.

CHAPTER 20

VIEWING OTHERS THROUGH THE WORD

Bible Reading: Mark 14–16

> "There came a woman with an alabaster vial of
> very costly perfume of pure nard; and she broke
> the vial and poured it over His head ... and
> they were scolding her. But Jesus said, 'Let her
> alone; ... she has done a good deed to Me'" (Mark
> 14:3, 5b–6).

Diet Dr Pepper! Our export store had worked a miracle. For the
first time in over two years, I put the blue and silver six-pack in
my grocery basket and began humming the American jingle as I
checked out. Spending more than I'd prepared for, I hummed a
little louder as I handed over several hundred Taiwan dollars to
the shopkeeper.

Every morning for the next six days, I put a cold "Pepper" in
a foam koozie before heading out the door to language school.
All the sudden, the Taiwan sky seemed brighter and the city
smelled more bearable. Instead of dreading class, I was taking on
a challenge and preparing for adventure.

The guard at the school entrance even seemed friendlier. Although
He spoke a different dialect from the one I was learning, we

exchanged pleasantries and I had found that he understood my Mandarin. Yes, I decided that I actually liked learning Chinese.

On Friday morning, I left home a little early in order to practice a few phrases with my new friend, the gate guard. As I approached, he smiled, nodded, and then pointed to my delicious drink. I returned the smile as I had learned the Mandarin word for "diet" just the day before.

"You really like Taiwan Beer?" he queried.

A little stunned, I managed to stammer, "What?!" wondering how he made his assumption.

"Taiwan Beer. It's good stuff. Even for breakfast!" He emphasized his approval with a knowing nod and a thumbs-up signal.

Realizing he was looking at my foam can holder, I sputtered my explanation. "Ke-luh, ke-luh" I said, repeating the Chinese word for cola over and again.

"It's a cola!" I finally blurted in English.

Interrupted by the ring of his phone, he laughed aloud and rolled his eyes. As he picked up the receiver, he dismissed me with a wink as if to say he'd keep my little secret. Realizing I'd been dismissed, I stumbled around the corner and into my classroom.

Somewhere between stressing fourth tone and learning the "ba" sentence pattern, I realized what had happened: the cans of the two drinks were remarkably similar. What the gate guard saw in my hand was the national drink of Taiwan. What I knew to be in the can was something quite different.

Jesus' view of the woman in today's reading was very different from that of the Pharisees. They regarded her actions outwardly. Jesus looked at what was going on inside (Mark 14:3–9).

We love to talk about being made into the image of God. It gives us value and allows us to hold our heads a little higher, especially after doing something really stupid. Yet, you and I aren't the only ones who the Lord prays for daily (John 17:20). Our world is full of all shapes and forms of Kingdom residents, not all of whom are easy for us to love. And knowing that we would feel this way, Jesus is still praying for our unity (John 17:21; Heb. 7:25).

When we regard one another here on earth, we are to do so according to the spirit, not according to the flesh (2 Cor. 5:16). We are to see past the outer man and look deep into the spirit of our brothers (1 Sam. 16:7). Kinda like taking a sip out of the can before knowing what is in it. *MAN LOOKS ON THE outward appearance GOD looks on the heart*

So what are we looking for inside of each other? How will we know when we've seen an evidence of the spirit, not the flesh? Here are a few basic guidelines of what to look for within your Kingdom siblings:

u shall speak to all who have skill I HAVE FILLED him with all knowledge

- A spirit of wisdom (Exod. 28:3; 31:3; Deut. 34:9)— an evidence of knowledge guided by Truth.
- A spirit of grace and supplication (Zech. 12:10)—an expression of forgiveness and prayerfulness.
- A spirit of truth (John 15:26; 1 John 4:6)—a filling of the Word.
- A spirit of holiness (Rom. 1:4)—a life like his heavenly Father.
- A spirit of life (Rom. 8:2)—a connection with eternity.
- A spirit of gentleness (1 Cor. 4:21; Gal. 6:1)—a tender endurance.
- A spirit of faith (2 Cor. 4:13)—a yielding to His Word.

When we see these traits within one another, we are glimpsing final reality, not just the here and now. We are training our eyes to focus on spiritual qualities instead of the glaring idiosyncrasies that can drive us crazy. Recognizing what's on the inside rather than what's on the outside allows us to see one another as Christ sees us—made into His image. Ask Him to open you spiritual eyes today.

Holy Father,

Thank You for looking at me through the eyes of Christ and seeing wisdom, righteousness, sanctification, and redemption in my life (1 Cor. 1:30). Somehow, in Your goodness, You have enriched me in both speech and knowledge; You even count me blameless in Christ (1 Cor. 1:5–8). Thank You for desiring my fellowship (1 Cor. 1:9).

Teach me how to look past the outer shell of my fellow man and see into their core. I am sorry for my jealousy. Give me Your viewpoint instead. May I be on the lookout for a spirit of holiness and gentleness within others and thus fulfill the law of Your love.

Give me a glimpse into my own heart, especially when I am prone to judge (Rom. 2:1). I've found that the very things that irritate me most about others are usually found inside me as well. Awaken me to discern the plank in my own eye instead of nit picking the speck in someone else's (Matt. 7:1–5).

I want to be a spirit observer. Open my eyes to recognize where You are working. As I recognize You in others, may I be drawn toward them in Your love. Thank You that with this simple action the world can know to whom I belong (John 13:35). In Jesus' name, Amen.

By this all will know u if you have love 4 1 another

CHAPTER 21

Know the Truth

DEPENDENCE ON THE WORD

Bible Reading: Luke 1–2

> "May it be done to me according to your Word" (Luke 1:38).

"Repeat after me."

Not my favorite three words. Well, at least not in language school. Yet, rote learning was highly valued at the Mandarin Daily-News Language Center, so I listened hard and reiterated well.

Shieh Lao Shr would start with the last bit of a sentence, speaking it slowly and then pausing for me to duplicate what I had heard. With each success, she added a phrase before it until I had faithfully reproduced an entire sentence. I found that if I understood each phrase, then I was more likely to use it outside of class in a real-life situation. Let's pick apart today's highlight verse and see if a little bit of repetition won't help us learn as well.

"Word"—Not only something spoken, this Word is expressed with such purity and perfection that the psalmist described the expression as sweet to the taste (Ps. 19:7–10). Jeremiah found this Word and professed this *dabar* caused his heart to sing with joy. Evidently, this Word is something to get excited about.

"Your Word"—This spiritually engrafted Word is not our own meaningless prattle, but God's Living Voice implanted within us by the Holy Spirit. His Word is actually Christ Himself, the very representation of God to man (James 1:21; Heb. 1:3). Like a hearty, healthy seed, His Word constantly bears fruit inside of us and spreads rapidly, even though we often don't realize it (Col. 1:6; 2 Thess. 3:1).

Because the Word is a living Person, He is always working to complete what He starts (Heb. 4:12; Ps. 138:8). Busy with never-ceasing activity, the Word is tirelessly accomplishing healing, freedom, and faith within each of His believers (Ps. 107:20, John 8:32; Rom. 10:17). The Word endures all of our ups and downs, powerfully reviving us when we don't "feel like it" anymore (1 Pet. 1:25; Ps. 119:154). His Word is power.

"According to Your Word"—Here we add a preposition, which expresses authority. Now we know the how; it is in compliance, or agreement, with the Word. The Greek *kata* or "according to" bears an idea of descending from the higher to the lower. Obviously, we know who is the higher.

"To me according to Your Word"—To me! I'm the lower one! Although I have faults and weaknesses, and "stumble in many ways," the Word is directed at me (James 3:2). Read it aloud and believe. This Word applies to you as well.

"Be it done to me according to Your Word"—This phrase "be it done" uses the same Greek word *ginomai* that John used to describe how the Word "was made" into flesh (John 1:14). Here, before the seed of the Word was placed into Mary's womb, she welcomed whatever generation of life the Spirit deemed worthy. "Let's go with it just as You said," she proclaimed. "Bring Your Word into existence inside of me (Rom. 4:17). I'm as ready as I'll ever be."

How often do we find our circumstances turn out according to what we have worried about rather than what He has promised?

Sometimes, we simply doubt ourselves into the worst possible scenario (Ps. 106:15). It is done according to our anxiety rather than according to His truth.

The emphasis, however, must be upon God, not on our fears. It's not a question of whether we've experienced a promise before. In fact, it is not a question at all. It's a statement, "Be it done" and must be fixed upon the dependability of God. As Paul well stated, "It does not depend on the man ... but on God" (Rom. 9:16).

God follows through with whatever He says (Isa. 46:10b; 55:11). In the same way that He spoke the world into existence, He is now speaking heaven's reality into existence within us. Didn't we just learn this to be Christ's secret of authority? God's promises animate into actuality when we believe Him. If we doubt His Word, we short-circuit the flow of His power. He still accomplishes His purpose—just not within the realm of the unbelieving (Heb. 4:2).

The choice is up to you. It will either be done to you according to your faith in His Word, or according to your doubt of His Word (Matt. 9:29). Choose you today whom you will serve: God or the realm of your own experience (Josh. 24:15). Decide that you will no longer give your mind the option of doubting what He says. In fact, why don't you repeat after me: "Lord, may it be done to me according to Your Word." Now let Him show You how to apply every promise that He reveals.

Holy Father,

What would my life look like if I really lived it according to Your Word? What if in financial crisis I said, "Be it done to me according to Your choice. You give and You take away. Either way, I'm going to bless Your name" (Job 1:21)? What if I lived Your Word with my family? "Be it done to us according to Your promise. I know that those who hopefully wait for You won't be put to shame. I'm going to continue seeking You daily on this matter" (Isa. 49:23). I desire to live Your Word among my neighbors. "Be it done to them according to Your Word. May

93

they receive the love of Truth, so that they may be saved" (2 Thess. 2:10).

Grant me the insight to hear what You are saying in every circumstance. I desire to join with Your prayers and open the very gates of heaven onto earth. Realizing that I usually pray for the physical, give me the desire to ask for the spiritual gifts that You have laid up and ready. Be it done to me according to Your Word. In Jesus' name, Amen.

CHAPTER 22

DISCERNMENT OF THE WORD

Bible Reading: Luke 3–5

> "And a voice came out of heaven, 'You are My beloved Son, in You I am well-pleased.'" (Luke 3:22).

> "And the devil said to Him, 'If You are the Son of God, tell this stone to become bread.'" (Luke 4:3).

LaVeta was our prayer warrior. When we arrived in Taichung, she and her husband, Bill, had already lived there for over twenty years. When I had a concern, LaVeta took it before the Lord. During her last year in Taiwan, the Lord called her to spend four hours alone with Him daily.

Through the years, LaVeta had collected a variety of Taiwanese handicrafts, one of which was a carved, wooden water buffalo. Resting on an end table in her living room, this three-foot-long ox had once been smoothly sanded to bring out the full grain of the camphor wood. One day, I asked her the history of the piece.

With a knowing glance at the beast, LaVeta began a story I'll never forget.

Crafted in SanYi, this water buffalo was acquired in LaVeta's first year in Taiwan. At that time in the 1970s, her home was

---

surrounded by this "living tractor of the east," which worked the nearby rice paddies. LaVeta chose this carved ox as a simple decorative piece to her Asian-styled home.

One day, while looking at her new purchase, LaVeta heard a voice within her head.

"Worship me for I am beautiful."

Startled and knowing that the idea did not originate within her, she replied to the beast, "You are not that beautiful!"

Somewhat panicked, she moved into her nearby kitchen to clear her head. "This couldn't be happening," she mused and prayed for the Lord to grant her peace. When her heart settled, she gingerly moved back within sight of the beast.

"Worship me for I am beautiful." This second time was as clear as the first.

Retreating again to the kitchen, LaVeta begged the Lord for guidance. In His wisdom, God revealed that this same power of evil actively influenced the Taiwanese every day, as they worshipped statues made from wood and stone. "Well, cast it away from our home," she pleaded, "and never let it bother anyone here again!"

With peace, LaVeta returned to the living room and looked boldly at the buffalo. Silent, the voice was never heard from again.

Although our "voices" may not be as definitive as the one LaVeta heard that day, we all struggle with the impressions within our heads. Hearing God speak to us doesn't silence the evil one from streaming his message as well. We must become as wise as serpents in this area and learn to discern between the voices that we hear daily (Matt. 10:16). Which voices come from within His Spirit and which are mere duplications of the world?

I've found the following three questions helpful in identifying the source of our impressions.

1. Is the voice I hear one of Truth (John 16:13) or accusation (Zech. 3:1)?

Satan's name actually means "the accuser" in Hebrew. Yet, we often allow his guilty, condemning thoughts to loop over and over within us. Christ tells us specifically that He didn't come into the world to blame, but in order that we might know salvation (John 3:17, KJV).

The Accuser weighs us down with guilt and negative thought patterns to steal our worship and destroy our praise (John 10:10). Entertaining daily pangs of self-reproach and negativity allows Satan to twist our focus off God rest it upon ourselves. On top of it all, the evil one somehow has convinced some of us that this attitude is actually one of true humility!

The Spirit of Truth, on the other hand, simply brings light on that which doesn't please the Father (John 3:20–21; 16:13). Once we understand Him, our response is to agree with God and quietly turn our desire back to Christ. Granted, we will come to the point again and again in our journey, but this repeated action was modeled by Christ Himself (1 Pet. 2:23). Go ahead. Allow His unconditional love to wash over you no matter what.

2. Does the voice give me peace (Ps. 29:11) or struggle (1 Cor. 3:3)?

The Father is all about blessing you with peace. However, many times the flesh's desires are so strong that we work ourselves into a frenzy to see them accomplished. James speaks clearly that a "wanter" is the very reason we are often so emotionally stirred-up (James 4:1–4). We are so bent upon satisfying the flesh's intense cravings that we easily forget the Lord. Dear friend, don't come to the point where you have satisfied that desire but are left with a lean soul (Ps. 106:15, KJV).

Find the time each day to quiet your personal longings before Him. Fasting is useful when these burnings are especially severe.

Seek His face, then begin movement in His direction. Always walk toward His peace (Ps. 34:14). *defeat form evil & do good seek peace + pursue it*

3. Will obeying the voice glorify Him (Matt. 5:16) or only glorify flesh (Phil. 3:3)? *Let your good works glorify God*
+ we are the true circumcision, who worship G. in spirit & glory in Christ
Because He is our sole source of peace and righteousness, God deserves due credit for these gifts. His dignity and reputation are above all and therefore He shares His glory with none (Isa. 42:8). In fact, seeking out your own fleshly glory will never quench the desire for more (Prov. 25:27). Seeking our flesh's kudos is not following after Him (John 5:41). *I AM THE LORD that is my name my glory I give 2 no other not my praise to*

I DO NOT receive glory from men

As you are well aware, recognizing the voice of Satan doesn't automatically shut him up. This comes by faith and practice. In my experience, it goes something like this:

God reveals that I have been listening to the evil one. I agree with the Lord's take on the situation and turn my focus back to Him. Usually, within minutes, a doubtful "but-what-about" thought will interrupt my peace.

I say, "Sorry, you are talking to the wrong person. I have no authority over this issue. Father, I bring this thought to You." Then, I offer either thanks or praise to God.

In the beginning, this peace may only last a few seconds. A sixty-day thought pattern is rarely erased immediately. But continue to drag this brooding captive back to the Lord where He can dismantle it (2 Cor. 10:5). Turn your focus onto peace and rest there. *we destroy arguments + every captive to the knowledge of God & take every*

Setting your mind on the Spirit is vital to life (Rom. 8:5–6). Do not be discouraged when you feel that you have done nothing but battle for two hours. This is part of the process. Remember, He is the one responsible for your growth. *knowledge of God*

You are a spiritual satellite, placed in orbit for a specific task. At any given moment, a multitude of sound waves comes your way.

Yet through practice, you come to recognize the source of each broadcast and disregard those from the evil one or the flesh. As God's receiver, desire then, to tune into the Father's frequency so that His thoughts may stream into you. And as His satellite, your life will then amplify His thoughts to those within your orbit.

Holy Father,

I have far too much noise in my head. Something is always louder than the sound of Your still small voice (1 Kings 19:11–12). Yet, I want to know You. I truly want to distinguish between guilt and truth; strife and peace; self-promotion and spiritual worship. Grant me discernment (Heb. 5:14).

May I come to know Your voice whether You speak amidst a burning bush or from the top of the mountain (Exod. 3:4; Exod. 19:20). Even when my eyes are prevented from recognizing You, may I sense Your Presence in spirit and follow by sharing with others (Luke 24:16, 31–33). Give me courage to know You through obedience, one day at a time (1 John 2:3). In Jesus' name, Amen.

one second at a time

By this way we know HIM if we keep His commands

CHAPTER 23

THE SEED OF THE WORD

Bible Reading: Luke 6–8

"The seed is the word of God" (Luke 8:11).

In order to postpone talking to four-year-old Mark about the birds and bees, his mom used a short tenable statement. "God plants a seed," she maintained. Each and every time Mark asked about her expanding waistline, she resorted back to her statement and sent him outside to play.

One night, alone in the tub, Mark reviewed the scuffs of the day. The scab on his knee reminded him of his fall off the fence. The dirt in his nails brought to mind the magnificent hole he'd dug. As he glanced at his stomach, he glimpsed something her couldn't quite place—a foreign object inside of his belly button.

After a little work, he dislodged the kernel and held it up for further scrutiny. Small, round, and grainlike, Mark wondered what it could be. Then, with sudden preschool inaccuracy, he deduced, "That was the seed that God planted! I've dug it out, and now I will never have children!"

God actually does plant a seed. He is the seed of His Word buried into every believer. When you "receive the word implanted" (James 1:21), you receive the very life of Christ, ready to perform

[handwritten: without God that u received the word of God not men which is at work in you]

His work in you (1 Thess. 2:13). Just as a seed houses the power of a new plant, His Word encases the very life of Jesus within (Heb. 1:3). And thankfully, He cannot be dislodged, mistakenly or otherwise.

Think about the last seed you held in your hand. Encased within that tiny seed coat was both a root and stem which, when full grown, will look like the plant from which it came. Given the proper temperature, oxygen, and water, that seed had the capacity to mature into a fruitful plant.

In the same way, a combination of faith, prayer, and the Holy Spirit will mature His seed within you into a healthy fruit-bearing life. And the great thing about His seed is that the growth is directed by God, not us (Col. 2:19). Our entire spiritual existence is His responsibility, not ours (1 Cor. 3:6). *[handwritten: I planted Apollos watered But God GAVE growth]*

No matter how we feel, His implanted seed is always living and active within us (Heb. 4:12). The seed may seem dormant during certain periods, but when conditions are favorable; His seed always bears visible fruit. You can bank on His promise that His Word always accomplishes His purposes (Isa. 55:10–11). *[handwritten: active 4 the word is living & sharp piercing soul & spirit discerning]*

You know, evangelism is not the only time that spiritual seed is sown. The mature fruit of the Spirit will reseed other areas of your life as well. For instance, you may bear true spiritual peace when faced with choosing a new church, but realize that the seed of peace has yet to sprout when it comes to choosing a mate. Resting in the peace that you do possess encourages growth in the areas that you lack.

Just as the farmer doesn't truly understand the growth of his crops, you will not always understand the mystery of increase within you (Mark 4:27). In the same way that you cannot worry yourself into growing taller, you also cannot direct your spiritual growth. Remember, this is the Father's business and His alone (1 Cor. 1:30). *[handwritten: HE is source of life in Christ whom god made wisdom righteousness + sanctification]*

You may find cycles of spiritual winter within you, in which everything seems dead. This too is His handiwork so that He may be glorified for His life-giving power. Don't worry, He specializes in calling the nonexistent into being (Rom. 4:17). Because you are only the soil, you don't have to be anxious about how fast you are growing. He is the seed implanted; He is the one who will bring it to fruition (1 Thess. 5:24).

Once again, your only response is the prayer of faith. No matter the season in which you find yourself, trust that He will perfect, confirm, strengthen, and establish His Word within you (1 Pet. 5:10). His discipline in your life is for the purpose of mending you and granting you calm consistency of mind. Even now, He is using your struggles to strengthen and stabilize your volatile soul.

Come on. Believe in the Gardener who is keeping and watering you "every moment" (Isa. 27:3). If a one-quarter-inch long seed can produce a 200-foot sequoia tree, surely His Word can produce the life of Christ within you. Even the giant redwoods didn't spring up in a day. Spiritual growth is a daily, gradual process of being renewed (Col. 3:10).

Thank Him for implanting the seed of the Word into your heart. Just as a small seed has the power to change the terrain around it, His Word is actively changing your heart. Give Him permission to till the soil of your heart, removing all rocks and thorns, so that the Spirit's growth in you has good soil. Ask Him to show you how to hold fast to His seed so that you may bear fruit with perseverance (Luke 8:15). There are those in good soil, hearing the word hold it fast in a good heart + bring forth fruit with patience

Holy Father,

I can't believe the power that lies within my very heart! The provision through Your Word is really quite mind boggling. Why don't I faithe You more? You have granted that I understand the mysteries of the Kingdom of God (Luke 8:10). Open my eyes so that I can see Your Word implanted within me.

I admit there have been times that I have believed You for a time and then grown lax in my faith (Luke 8:13). Fleshly anxiety demanded more of my mind than following You. I'm most ashamed to confess that most often my disregard for Your Word comes through seeking my fleshly gratification through entertainment and amusements. My fleshly indulgence brings no peace and effectually strangles evidence of Your active work within me (Luke 8:14).

Thank You for already removing the rocks and the thorns, so that my heart's soil may be ready for growth. Grant me the moisture of Your Spirit and Your gentle watch-care, O Faithful Farmer. Allow me the good soil that makes way for the infinite root system of the Spirit's growth within. I am here for You. Hold me fast. In Jesus' name, Amen.

CHAPTER 24

WAITING ON THE WORD

Bible Reading: Luke 9–11

> "Mary, who was seated at the Lord's feet, listening
> to His word" (Luke 10:39).

Throughout the years of our marriage, Mark has teased me regarding my impatience. I suppose that it began when I interrupted his marriage proposal to pop my own question. Or maybe it started when I called to let him know that I was going to the jeweler's to pick up my engagement ring by myself (which, by the way, he did *not* allow me to do ... but that is another story altogether!).

Despite the Lord's call to bear fruit (John 15:16), patience remains the smallest and hardest to harvest from the branches of my life. For years, I equated this fruit of the Spirit with the pomegranate: hard to peel with far too many seeds. Yet, the Lord began to reveal this attitude for what it was—a fleshly stance against waiting on God. Within a week of this wake-up call, God gave me a laboratory pop-quiz in an overcrowded Chinese airport.

Early in our overseas experience, I had learned that queuing necessitates pointy elbows and brute force. Yet, on this particular day, I continued to hear the Lord say, "Yield to them, yield to

Me." As one after another inserted themselves into my space in line, I comforted myself smugly knowing I was following His lead. But when we arrived at the ticket counter to find our flight reservations given away altogether, the blood began to pulse in my ears. I figured I'd been patient long enough!

As Mark calmly talked to the agent, I pulled away for a quick prayer: "Lord, make them give us a seat!" Although the prayer wasn't mirroring the one that He was praying, He did answer me: "You said you wanted to fertilize the fruit of patience. Your waiting today will be on Me, not on the airline." And for the next ten hours in a China airport, I explored how to wait on the Lord, while unable to do much else.

Waiting on Him should be the lifestyle of every believer, but we seldom stop to practice this discipline. Our English word *wait* is actually of Germanic origin meaning, "to watch." So, rather than some passive state of just hanging loose, waiting on God means expectantly watching for "God signals" all throughout our day.

Waiting is actually good for us as it strengthens our spiritual muscle of faith. In Isaiah 40:31 we read, "Those who wait for the LORD will gain new strength." Within this Hebrew word for "wait," we find the idea of binding together by twisting. Like a thin sapling entwining around a mature tree, we are to be ever twisting and turning toward the Lord. From the perspective of the sapling, the process seems endless—ever spiraling, but going nowhere. Yet, as the sapling continues bending and wrapping, it actually follows the path of the trunk. The course of this tender shoot will not overlap onto itself, but ever so slowly, will continue upward with the direction of the tree. In time, if the seedling depends closely upon the trunk, the two will actually fuse together to share nutrients, water, and light.

We are no different. As one with our Lord, we must learn to wait upon Him. This is the Father's chosen method to unite our life with His. Active waiting involves pausing, moment by moment, to refocus upon His Presence within.

This is no self-dependent growth. Although fleshly confidence stagnates our growth, active waiting keeps us flexible—always bending and moving in the direction that He leads. Andrew Murray, a nineteenth-century missionary, said it best: "The whole duty and blessedness of waiting on God … is … that we … cannot for any time come into contact with Him without that life and power silently, secretly beginning to enter into us and blessing us"[5]

God desires us to focus our waiting upon Him. "My soul, wait in silence for God only, for my hope is from Him" (Ps. 62:5). We are not waiting until we get out of school or waiting to get married. We are not waiting to get a better job or to stop working altogether. The focus of our waiting is not in the beginning or ending of something, but in the Word Himself.

Every time I am forced to wait, even on something as simple as a phone call or an elevator, it is God speaking to me. He is signaling me to look for Him. Where have I seen evidence of Him or what word would He recall to my mind? Spiritual waiting strengthens our faith.

Today, allow Christ to reframe your understanding of waiting. Determine to rest in Him, using every opportunity to bend toward Him. Every grocery line or traffic delay presents you a chance to wait, not on others, but on Him. Be proactive to use fragments of time while "on-hold" to watch for His indicators. When your flight is delayed or the repairman never shows, focus your attention back to Him. See this time as His reminder, accentuating your fusion with Him as you turn toward His Word. Practicing this action daily is healthy and always results in His favor (Lam. 3:25–26). Try it and see.

. The Lord is good to those who wait + Him - 2 the soul that seeks Him.

---

5 Andrew Murray, *Waiting on God* (Springdale, PA: Whitaker House, 1983), 41.

Holy Father,   *Before any of us*

I exalt You because You are worth waiting for. Before I was ever born, You were making plans and carrying them out in perfect faithfulness (Isa. 25:1). That's pretty astounding!

I want to come to the place where I can get excited with Isaiah and say, "Wow! This is our God for whom we have waited!" (Isa. 25:9). Yet, for the most part, my prayers are filled with the words like "quickly," "soon," and "now."

I confess my lack of patience. For years, I have smoothed over it as no big deal, but now I see that in reality, patience is as much of Your character as goodness (Gal. 5:22). Teach me how to wait for You (Ps. 25:5). Remind me of this lesson every time I'm in line at the store or holding on the phone. Allow me to reframe life's interruptions as a training time to wait for You. Keep my eyes not on the people who cause the hold-up, but on You, who are worthy of the wait. In order to do this, I'm going to need Your patience, not my own. Mine will never be enough. In Jesus' name, Amen.

CHAPTER 25

APPROVAL AND THE WORD

Bible Reading: Luke 12–15

> "If anyone comes to Me, and does not hate his
> own father and mother and wife and children and
> brothers and sisters, yes, and even his own life, he
> cannot be My disciple" (Luke 14:26).

As overseas living became more the norm, I gradually made the
shift from my American culture to the host culture I lived within.
I learned not only to take my shoes off before entering homes but
also the value of doing so in my own home. I became an avid
recycler and grew to love shopping in the local market.

Yet what began as a simple cultural transition shifted at some
point to something much more dangerous. In desiring to fit into
my new host home, I allowed my motivation to shift from the
Lord to the approval of man. During a very memorable quiet
time, the Lord asked a very haunting question: "Kandy, are you
trying to win My approval or man's?"

Remembering I had actually read this somewhere in the Word,
I thumbed for the reference to read the actual verse. I found it in
black and white among Paul's explanation to the Galatian church.

"If I were still trying to please men, I would not be a bond-servant of Christ" (Gal. 1:10).

What I had thought was my desire to please God was actually flesh's desire to please sin.

Over the next several months, the Lord continued to reveal His truth regarding this temptation. I wanted to hear His voice and wait patiently for Him, but I had to honestly admit that I often sought out the praise of others. I wanted to be like Jesus, but my flesh wanted to have others like me. Slowly, I began to see how this was of the flesh and, therefore, nauseating to the Lord (Luke 16:15).

Doubtless, Jesus Himself knew the Proverb that searching out one's own glory doesn't result in true prestige (Prov. 25:27). But, He also knew that looking manward shuts off the flow of faith. A heart either is turned to believe in God or will direct toward the approval of man. "How do you think you could possibly faith when your heart is filling up with glory from another source?" Jesus asked (John 5:44). *How can u believe who seek glory from one another but not the glory of God*

When we are weak in faith, we can most often trace it directly back to this source. Choosing man's admiration honors fleshly opinions. It's like turning completely around to hear a conversation behind you, when God is speaking to you face to face. Looking to man for recognition takes our eyes off Christ, who not only tattooed faith onto your heart but is also willing to spend the rest of your lifetime filling in the details (Heb. 12:2).

Without faith, our flesh is caught between trying to please others and making sure they please us. What begins as a simple act of wanting to share happiness can turn the people-pleaser into an exacting person who is never pleased. People-pleasers can become easily provoked as they feel they "do so much for others with nothing in return." Note, this is the exact opposite of love (1 Cor. 13:5). *love*

love not arrogant or rude does not insist upon its own way it is not irritable or resentful

Being a man-pleaser not only diminishes our faith but also lowers the quality of disciple that we can produce. Just as a slave is no greater than his master is (John 15:20), a disciple will initially assume the characteristics of the one he admires. If we are constantly stumbling over our own need to be approved by others, then those we disciple may head straight down the same path. May we be servants who model the transforming power of the presence of Christ rather than reproduce our own desire for distinction (Matt. 23:15).

In your time of reflection, prayerfully consider the following chart, asking the Lord to reveal to you where you most usually reside. As He reveals attitudes or characteristics that are not pleasing, remember that change only comes as He performs it within you. Allowing Him to transform you may involve actual personality changes in some areas.

God Pleaser   Flesh Pleaser

God Pleaser	Flesh Pleaser
Serves the Lord (Col. 3:23)	Busy pleasing others (Gal. 1:10)
Receives people God brings their way (John 6:37)	Loves accumulating things (Matt. 6:24;1 John 2:15–16)
Interested in thinking His thoughts (Ps. 104:34)	Consumed with their own body or health (Matt. 6:25)
Hungry for truth (Jer. 15:16; Matt. 5:6)	Enslaved to their own appetite (Rom. 16:18; Phil. 3:19)
Spiritually minded (Rom. 8:6; 2 Cor. 5:7)	Concerned for the fleshly (Rom. 8:7–8)
Labors over others in prayer (Col. 4:12)	Worries over their own needs (Luke 10:40–41)
Familiar with truth (2 Tim. 2:15)	Comfortable with worldly small talk (2 Tim. 2:16)

Doesn't allow the flesh to initiate actions (John 5:30; 8:28–29)	Places confidence in their flesh (Phil. 3:3)
Loves the Father's words (Jer. 15:16)	Fears the words of others (1 Sam. 15:24)
Learns through their suffering (Heb. 5:8)	Grumbles and complains (Phil. 3:14)
Never trust's in man's opinion, but God's (John 2:24–25; 1 Cor. 4:5)	Loves the approval of others (John 12:43)
Interested in issues of the heart (2 Cor. 5:12)	Prideful of appearance (2 Cor. 5:12)
Receives their critique from God alone (1 Cor. 4:4)	Needs to justify their actions to others (Luke 16:15)

Holy Father,

You've spoken clearly regarding where my affections should lie. I confess to You I've stumbled into pleasing others. I'm sorry that I have sought man's approval rather than Your own (John 12:43). Now, I realize the reason for my shallow faith.

Release the Holy Spirit to renew the spirit of my mind to learn what is pleasing to You (Eph. 4:23; 5:10). May this regeneration overflow my soul into my actions, so that I may also speak words that please You (1 Thess. 2:4). You know that I find this harder in some places than others, Father. Grant me the singular desire to please You no matter where I am (2 Cor. 5:9).

I give You permission to remind me throughout my day about this commitment. Send Truth quickly when I try to justify my actions before others or grumble when someone's actions don't please me. Prompt my mind with Scriptures that reveal how I can best cause You delight (Col. 1:10). Allow me to practice Your presence. In Jesus' name, Amen.

Be renewed in spirit of mind

BE renewed in the spirit of our minds lead a life worthy of the LORD. bearing fruit in every good work + increasing in knowledge of God

CHAPTER 26

KINGDOM LIVING AND THE WORD

Bible Reading: Luke 16–19

> "For behold, the kingdom of God is in your midst" (Luke 17:21).

From the Waverly wall border to Mark's extra-long recliner, our Taiwanese apartment retained a little piece of Americana. We listened to English music and read old copies of *Southern Living* magazine circulated within the ex-pat community. My recipes mirrored my mother's so our kitchen smelled of casseroles and hot bread more often than stir-fry and rice. Every sight, sound, and smell testified that "foreigners" lived in our building.

Did you realize that as a Kingdom citizen, your spirit is occupied by the Holy Foreigner to this world? But unlike my Taiwanese apartment, Christ's tabernacle is not just surface decor. When He moves into a life, He bulldozes the entirety of the old, clearing out even the soil on which it rested. Christ's residence in you is altogether heavenly and new (Acts 7:48; 2 Cor. 5:17).

Unfortunately, we keep looking at the shadow of the old structure. We think that since we can still see the same form of facial features, we are doomed to keep acting the same. Nothing could

112

be further from the truth. Just because it seems impossible to us, doesn't mean it's impossible to God.

So why did the Father renew our entire inner man and leave us with such an annoying body?

For one thing, it's about hope. Mysteriously, this expectation of the future is how we draw near to God (Heb. 7:19). Just think. *Law made nothing perfect* Without hope, we wouldn't anticipate the pleasure of a deeper relationship with Him. Hope is the actual cord that keeps drawing us toward His glory (Heb. 6:19).

I have to admit; sometimes the walk of faith is like teetering on a tightrope in the dark. Perched high above the ground, every step seems shaky and we pray the weather doesn't get worse. We feel our way, wondering just when the sun will come up.

Yet, in every situation, hope is our guide-wire. Anchored firmly within Christ, hope is our stability and the direction we move as we edge toward final reality. Keeping a steady grip on hope and our eyes on Jesus actually results in the ongoing purity of soul that we are so hungry for (1 John 3:3). *Everyone who hopes in Jesus purifies Himself*

Within our flesh, soul, and spirit, our fleshly bodies are in a state of daily decay (2 Cor. 4:16). Taking up Christ within our spirits only increases our longing to get rid of the futility we feel toward the flesh. Paul himself said that dealing with his body literally made him groan (2 Cor. 5:2). It's really not surprising that you and I have the same feeling. In fact, all of creation deals with this same frustration (Rom. 8:20).

Our victory is living an inside-out life.

Perfection in Christ is a state that He has already achieved within you. His obedience made you righteous, not your obedience to the Law (Rom. 5:19). The reason that He rebuilt us from the ground up was in order to break the power line from our soul to our flesh (Rom. 6:6). Accepting His death as ours effectively plugs our thoughts and emotions into this new source of power driven by hope. Instead of helplessly walking toward the flesh, the thoughts and emotions of our soul turn to edge toward the spirit.

We've been duped into believing that "good Christians" finally "get it right." In all reality, "good Christians" just finally stop looking at the situation with fleshly eyes. We stop our own striving and let His Spirit deal with our flesh. I love the way Chinese Christian Watchman Nee describes it:

"Lord, I cannot do it; therefore I will no longer try to do it. Lord, I cannot, therefore I will take my hands off; from now on I trust Thee for that."

We refuse to act, we depend on Him to do so, and then we enter joyfully and fully into the action He initiates. It is not passivity, it is a most active life, trusting the Lord like that; drawing life from Him, taking Him to be our very life, letting Him live His life in us as we go forth in His name."[6]

There is a Power working mightily within the center of all you are (Col. 1:29). This Energy has nothing to do with who you are or who you have been. The strength of Christ oozes forth from you simply because He chose to do so once you became His child. And better yet, this Holy Energy Source has a specific purpose: constantly enabling you to deny ungodliness (Titus 2:11–12). So take your hands off the guide-wire connecting your soul to the flesh. That direction is a dead line anyway. Instead, ask Him to place your hand directly onto His hope that surges power through you. Live from the inside out, and even your body will begin to look, sound, and smell like a Kingdom resident in a foreign land.

---

6 Watchman Nee, *The Normal Christian Life* (Fort Washington, PA: Christian Literature Crusade, 1973), 124.

Dear Holy Father,

Thank You for moving the entire Kingdom of God to live within me (Luke 17:21). Because of You, I no longer have to be carried off by evil, but now I can overcome evil with good (Rom. 12:21). That's pretty cool. *overcome evil with Good*

You have authority over my flesh, but I admit, I often hold onto flesh too tightly (John 17:2). I'm just not sure how to let go of this part of me that is already dead, but I know that You are calling me to do so. In hope, I faithe Your ability to accomplish it in me (1 Thess. 5:24). Go for it. *GOSPEL come not just within but in soul*

I'm sure there will be times that I will find my hand on the flesh before I realize what I've done. In those situations, give me the insight as to how to lead this unruly animal back to Your feet for sacrifice (Rom. 12:1). Truly, I'd rather have You deal with it, rather than keep feeding it myself.

I want to live an inside-out life—the kind where Your Spirit does the living instead of me. Direct me to grasp firmly the hope of the Spirit. May my face time with the flesh decrease, so that Your countenance within me is increased (John 3:30). I love you.

CHRIST HAS PWR 2 overcome NT ME

HE must increase, I must decrease

CHAPTER 27

PURIFICATION AND THE WORD

Bible Reading: Luke 20–22

> "Simon, Simon, behold, Satan has demanded permission to sift you like wheat; but I have prayed for you, that your faith may not fail" (Luke 22:31–32).

In many parts of Asia, grain is still winnowed by hand. The same men and women, who hover by the glow of their television each night, manually toss grain into the sun's glare each day. This method has changed little since Jesus discussed the process with Peter two thousand years ago.

Before separating the chaff from the wheat, the stalk must be sliced from the plant and carried to the threshing floor. There, cattle trample the reeds, separating the heads from the straw and then loosening the chaff around the grain. Once the grain is broken, workers toss the crop into the breeze where the husks are carried away and the heavier wheat berry bounces back to the threshing floor.

Up until the wheat is ready to be used, the straw and the chaff are vital elements in the growth of the grain. Without them, the wheat kernel could never survive. The stalk supports the head, both off the ground and toward the sun, while the husk protects the tender grain from the heat and pests. Yet, to realize the true purpose of the wheat, it must be separated, broken, and sifted.

We are no different. The passage we have just read in Luke 22 wasn't spoken to Peter alone. The two words translated "you" in our English versions were actually plural in the original Greek. Satan not only asked for Peter on his pitchfork, but also for every Christian to come.

Satan's sifting sometimes comes in the form of monotonous bouncing against the screen of life's tedious duties. At other times, a violent upheaval sends you free falling onto the threshing floor to await the next assault. Indeed, our adversary attempts to use "permission to sift" as a way to steal, kill, and destroy (John 10:10). *The thief comes to steal, I come that he might have abundant life*

This could paralyze us with fear. But wait—let's faithe it through. While our accuser has requested permission to shake us, Jesus Himself has also made a request on our behalf. He didn't pray that we would remain immovable or perfect in every instance. Instead, He asked that, in spite of our circumstances, our faith remain immovable (Luke 22:32). *I prayed 4 u your faith may not fail - turn strengthen ur Brethren*
From our way of thinking, Peter did fail. He failed in courage, in devotion, and in passion. Yet, from God's perspective, this shaking worked to rid Peter of the unnecessary chaff of selfish zeal. Before Peter received a faith that wouldn't fail, he had to walk straight through one of the darkest hours of his life. The Father allowed Peter to see just how helpless he was to fulfill his own vows. Like Peter, the paths of righteousness often take us first through the valley of death to the flesh (Ps. 23:3–4). Our motivation must not be in how we are perceived, but in how we persevere.

While the 7.6 earthquake vibrated through the walls of my seventh-floor apartment, I didn't pray that the tremor would stop. I prayed desperately that we would live through it. In the middle of a crisis, you beg for life, not just help.

After the dust settled, we began to understand why our twenty-five-story building withstood the violence. It was all about the materials within the structure. Our building was constructed with flexible steel frames that actually embraced the shaking. As these frames rocked up and down, the jolts were absorbed within twisted steel cables that allowed movement, but not collapse. We were overjoyed to find that our apartment was actually built with such a quake in mind.

In Luke 22:32, the Greek for "fail" is the word *ekleipo* from which we get our English verb "eclipse." In essence, Jesus prayed that our conviction of His presence would never be blocked from sight. During the dark siftings of life, we may find it difficult to see Him clearly, but no crisis can obscure the light of who we've known Him to be.

You and I will endure times of shaking because our Father knows our flesh has built up attitudes and habits that are juxtaposed to knowing Him (2 Cor. 10:5). Simply put, there is still a lot of chaff sticking to our wheat. Our God allows the adversary to agitate our lives so that we may be separated from all that is not Kingdom strong. He removes those things which can be shaken "so that those things which cannot be shaken may remain" (Heb. 12:27).

Our Builder designed us with the sifting in mind. He granted Satan permission because He knew we could handle it. No trial that comes to you will ever be larger than what you are built to withstand (1 Cor. 10:13). You were created with the flexibility to embrace the shaking. This is not to say that you won't groan and creak as our apartment did during the earthquake. And like our building, you may see some of your cosmetic facade broken and ruined. But faith that depends upon Christ, instead of religion, is never eclipsed completely.

Take some time today to think through past times of crisis. Whether your sifting was brutal or merely tedious, remember specific ways that He restored your confidence in His faithfulness.

We know that in every-thing God works 4 good 4 those who love Him

Don't dwell on the items you still don't understand, but on the good that He has brought about despite the trial (Rom. 8:28). Speak out your thankfulness for the positive that resulted in past siftings. Remember that your faith doesn't only involve belief in Him, but trust that He rewards you as well (Heb. 11:6).

Holy Father,

Thank You for always knowing ahead of time what I will need. It's such a relief to know that despite my feelings, You've built me strong in spirit. Indeed, if it had not been for Your gift of faith, I know that I would have collapsed into despair (Ps. 27:13).

I have to agree with Peter—a life of salvation, although free, isn't easy (1 Pet. 4:18). At times, I boast of my own faithfulness and then scramble when I am sifted. Grant me to see that my trials are worth the pain. Reveal how my sufferings become a holy offering; something I can return to You in the form of praise, glory, and honor (1 Pet. 1:6–7). *Rejoice thru suffering*

I also need to see what good the shaking does for my here and now. You promised that if I believe, even when I can't see You, You will give me inexpressible joy and the ability to experience Your hidden value of excellence (1 Pet. 1:8). Save me from my vacillating soul (1 Pet. 1:9). Boy, do I need that! *UR. Faith is tested u your sak.*

I realize that I will be sifted. The slanderer of my soul roams about seeking a chink in my faith (1 Pet. 5:8). I ask that You rescue me from temptation and teach me how to plant my will firmly against him, so as to oppose his every move (2 Pet. 2:9; 1 Pet. 5:9). At the same time, I want to turn my gaze so that I fix my hope completely on Your face (1 Pet. 1:13). *Set UR Hope upon grace given 2 u*

Don't forget what You promised after the sifting. You promised to mend me into Your perfect form; to give my mind the peace of consistency; and to strengthen and stabilize my soul (1 Pet. 5:10). I give You dominion both today and forever, Amen (1 Pet. 5:11).

CHAPTER 28

MOVING FORTH IN THE WORD

Bible Reading: Luke 23–24

> "And behold, I am sending forth the promise of My Father upon you" (Luke 24:49).

> "You will make me full of gladness with Your presence" (Acts 2:28).

We've been on a journey together haven't we? Know that I've prayed for you every step of the way. Although this is the last chapter, neither one of us is at the end, but at a new beginning. We've shared, laughed, and maybe even cried, none of which escaped the Word.

As you go from here, do so with the confidence that you've been anointed with wisdom from the Holy One (1 John 2:20). You know what to do next because the powerful Word teaches you about all things (1 John 2:27). I believe in You. He does too.

Holy Father,

Speaking to Your people has always been a priority to You, huh? First, You used prophets as Your mouthpiece and now You just speak directly through Your Son (Heb. 1:1–2). The

120

1 Pet. His power granted us all things that pertain to life & godliness through the knowledge of HIM who called us to his glory —

astounding part is that You have adopted me as Your child and actually desire to speak to me. What an honor! *I AM Honored*

Becoming my life as You have, I've discovered that moment by moment You generate into me everything that I need for the activity, aims, and acts of godliness (2 Pet. 1:3). You didn't adopt me and then abandon me to fend for myself. In fact, Your adoption actually included changing my spiritual DNA. You called and excellence sprung into existence within me. You spoke and glory reflected into my very soul (2 Pet. 1:3). I am truly grateful.

Somehow, deep within, You built a new kind of dwelling place, able to accommodate more than just three dimensions. Not only is Christ in me, but somehow at the same time, I'm with Him in the heavenlies as well (2 Tim. 1:14; Eph. 2:6). Because of You, my own spirit emanates with power, love, and sound judgment regardless of what I'm thinking or feeling (2 Tim. 1:7). Christ is being formed in me. *GOD did not give us a spirit of timidity but of pwr love self-control*

In my early understanding of You, I misunderstood all of the talk about the law. I thought that as a Christian, I needed to achieve to the point of getting it all right. Sometimes the law was in the form of religiosity; sometimes it was in the form of how my parents raised me; and then sometimes it was a blend of my own expectations of both. How little I understood You.

No matter what self-effort looks like in my life, it never makes me right with You (Rom. 3:20). Sure, You used those rules to lead me directly up to You, but in essence those guidelines aren't You (Gal. 3:24). When we get inside You we find that You are actually the end of legalistic living (Rom. 10:4). The whole reason that I went through all of those self-made regulations was to realize that I needed more than that (Rom. 5:20). Thank You for being much, much more! *no human will B justified by the law* *Christ is end of LAW* *where sin increased, grace abounded all the more*

Now that I comprehend just a little of *who* I am, I need You to constantly hit the refresh button of my soul. Bad habits die hard, and I find that I assume control of my decisions. Remind me often that, in You, I am the righteousness of God (2 Cor. 5:21). And as such, I don't need self-made religion. The law was made for the unrighteous, not me (1 Tim. 1:9). *He made Him to B sin who knew no sin, so that in Him we might become Righteous. of God*

IF WE LIVE By the Spirit Let us also walk by the Spirit.

Kandy Persall

we live by the spirit

Since I am no longer under the law, I'm ready to walk in the Spirit (Gal. 5:18). After all, I do live in the Spirit. Teach me then to take each step that way, too (Gal. 5:25). You promised that sin doesn't have to be my master, so let's run together in the freedom of grace (Rom. 6:14). Sin has no dominion over ME

I believe that You are bigger than my doubts. Grant me lots of faith because that's what keeps me out of trouble (Rom. 14:23) I'm ready. Let's go.

whatever does not proceed from faith IS SIN

Why do we doubt God — Because we forget it isn't about doubting God but ourselves not what goes into the mouth of man but what comes ou OF THE MOUTH

out of mouth come evil thoughts murder adultery fornication theft false witness, slander.

122

EPILOGUE

Has being in His Word increased your hunger for more of Him? I sure hope so.

So just where do you go next? I have a suggestion. You have just completed reading through the Gospels. Why not put this book aside and commit to read through the entire New Testament next month?

Now don't freak out. Remember, you aren't reading to get something out of it, but to allow the Living Word plenty of time to speak to you. You'll be surprised to find that within the first week, the Word will begin to show up in unexpected places in your daily life.

Since I believe you are up for the challenge, I'm including a guideline below as a template. According to how quickly you read, this should take you somewhere between 30-45 minutes a day, far less than most of us spend on the internet. Start on the first of a month, so that you can easily keep up with where you should be on any given day. I suggest that you do this two months in a row, since there are bound to be days that you won't be able to finish it all in one sitting.

1. Matthew 1-9
2. Matthew 10-16
3. Matthew 17-23
4. Matthew 24-28

5. Mark 1-7
6. Mark 8-16
7. Luke 1-6
8. Luke 7-11
9. Luke 12-18
10. Luke 19-24
11. John 1-6
12. John 7-12
13. John 13-21
14. Acts 1-7
15. Acts 8-14
16. Acts 15-21
17. Acts 22-28
18. Romans 1-8
19. Romans 9-16
20. 1 Corinthians 1-9
21. 1 Corinthians 10-16
22. 2 Corinthians
23. Galatians –Ephesians
24. Philippians – 1 Thessalonians
25. 2 Thessalonians – Philemon
26. Hebrews
27. James – 1 Peter
28. 2 Peter - Jude
29. Revelation 1-12
30. Revelation 13-22

I AM THE ALPHA & OMEGA

This is going to rock your world. I can't wait to hear how He has spoken to you. I'd love to hear your victories and insights via the web at www.hungryformore.org. Or maybe my daughter, Hilary and I can come to your location for a Hungry For More retreat. Either way, I'm eager to hear what the Father is saying just to you.

ABOUT THE AUTHOR

Kandy Persall and her husband, Mark, spent twenty years living as foreigners in Asia. She has a bachelor's degree in communication from Texas Tech University and a Mandarin certificate from the Jin Shin Huei Language Institute of Taipei, Taiwan. She now travels to churches throughout the United States speaking at women's conferences to help women find what they are truly hungry for.

Kandy and Mark make their home in Lubbock, Texas. They are parents of two adult daughters, who are vitally involved in her ministry. Their oldest daughter, Hannah, was not only the creative force behind the website, but also produced the cover design of this book. Hilary, their youngest, leads worship at many of Kandy's conferences.

good don't participate can't get royalties anyway

CPSIA information can be obtained at www.ICGtesting.com
Printed in the USA
LVOW062338100113

315240LV00001B/3/P